FYODOR DOSTOEVSKY

EDITED AND WITH AN
INTRODUCTION BY HAROLD BLOOM

CURRENTLY AVAILABLE

BLOOM'S
MAJOR NOVELISTS

Jane Austen
The Brontës
Willa Cather
Stephen Crane
Charles Dickens
Fyodor Dostoevsky
William Faulkner
F. Scott Fitzgerald
Thomas Hardy
Nathaniel Hawthorne
Ernest Hemingway
Henry James
James Joyce
Franz Kafka
D. H. Lawrence
Herman Melville
Toni Morrison
Marcel Proust
John Steinbeck
Stendhal
Leo Tolstoy
Mark Twain
Alice Walker
Edith Wharton
Virginia Woolf

FYODOR DOSTOEVSKY

EDITED AND WITH AN INTRODUCTION
BY HAROLD BLOOM

© 2003 by Chelsea House Publishers, a subsidiary of
Haights Cross Communications.

A Haights Cross Communications Company

Introduction © 2003 by Harold Bloom.

All rights reserved. No part of this publication may be reproduced
or transmitted in any form or by any means without the written
permission of the publisher.

Printed and bound in the United States of America.

First Printing
1 3 5 7 9 8 6 4 2

Library of Congress Cataloging-in-Publication Data
Fyodor Dostoevsky / edited and with an introduction by Harold Bloom.
   p. cm. —(Bloom's major novelists)
  Includes bibliographical references and index.
  ISBN 0-7910-6346-1
   1. Dostoyevsky, Fyodor, 1821–1881—Criticism and interpretation—
  Handbooks, manuals, etc. 2. Dostoyevsky, Fyodor, 1821–1881—
   Examinations—Study guides. I. Bloom, Harold. II. Series.
PG3328.Z6 F96 2002
 891.73'3—dc21   2002014666

Chelsea House Publishers
1974 Sproul Road, Suite 400
Broomall, PA 19008-0914

www.chelseahouse.com

Contributing Editor: Emmy Chang

Produced by: www.book*designing*.com

Cover design by Robert Gerson

Contents

User's Guide	7
Editor's Note	8
Introduction	9
Biography of Fyodor Dostoevsky	12
Plot Summary of *Crime and Punishment*	15
List of Characters in *Crime and Punishment*	19
Critical Views on *Crime and Punishment*	21
George Gibian on Symbolism and the Epilogue	21
Edward Wasiolek on the Plot	23
W. D. Snodgrass on the Women and the Mare	25
Pierre R. Hart on the Narrator	27
W. Woodin Rowe on Antinomy	29
Mikhail Bakhtin on Carnival	31
W. J. Leatherbarrow on Porfiry	33
A. D. Nuttall on Svidrigailov	36
Plot Summary of *The Idiot*	38
List of Characters in *The Idiot*	42
Critical Views on *The Idiot*	44
F. F. Seeley on Nastasya	44
Roger L. Cox on Execution, Epilepsy, and Apocalypse	46
Michael Holquist on Teleology	48
Elizabeth Dalton on Dostoevsky and the Unconscious	50
Plot Summary of *Demons* (*The Possessed*)	53
List of Characters in *Demons* (*The Possessed*)	57
Critical Views on *Demons* (*The Possessed*)	59
Philip Rahv on Russia's *Demons*	59
Vyacheslav Ivanov on Marya	61
John Jones on "At Tikhon's"	63
N. N. Shneidman on Suicide and Freedom	65
René Girard on Myshkin, Stavrogin, and the Underground	67
Plot Summary of *The Brothers Karamazov*	70
List of Characters in *The Brothers Karamazov*	74
Critical Views on *The Brothers Karamazov*	76

R. P. Blackmur on Guilt	76
Robert L. Belknap on the Narrative	78
Richard Peace on Dmitri's Punishment	80
Malcolm V. Jones on the Grand Inquisitor	81
Robert Louis Jackson on Ivan's Rebellion	84
Valentina A. Vetlovskaya on Alyosha	86
Roger B. Anderson on Zosima and Karamazov	88
Works by Fyodor Dostoevsky	91
Works about Fyodor Dostoevsky	93
Acknowledgments	97
Index of Themes and Ideas	100

User's Guide

This volume is designed to present biographical, critical, and bibliographical information on the author's best-known or most important works. Following Harold Bloom's editor's note and introduction is a detailed biography of the author, discussing major life events and important literary accomplishments. A plot summary of each novel follows, tracing significant themes, patterns, and motifs in the work.

A selection of critical extracts, derived from previously published material from leading critics, analyzes aspects of each work. The extracts consist of statements from the author, if available, early reviews of the work, and later evaluations up to the present. A bibliography of the author's writings (including a complete list of all works written, cowritten, edited, and translated), a list of additional books and articles on the author and his or her work, and an index of themes and ideas in the author's writings conclude the volume.

Harold Bloom is Sterling Professor of the Humanities at Yale University and Henry W. and Albert A. Berg Professor of English at the New York University Graduate School. He is the author of over 20 books, including *Shelley's Mythmaking* (1959), *The Visionary Company* (1961), *Blake's Apocalypse* (1963), *Yeats* (1970), *A Map of Misreading* (1975), *Kabbalah and Criticism* (1975), *Agon: Toward a Theory of Revisionism* (1982), *The American Religion* (1992), *The Western Canon* (1994), and *Omens of Millennium: The Gnosis of Angels, Dreams, and Resurrection* (1996). *The Anxiety of Influence* (1973) sets forth Professor Bloom's provocative theory of the literary relationships between the great writers and their predecessors. His most recent books include *Shakespeare: The Invention of the Human*, a 1998 National Book Award finalist, and *How to Read and Why*, which was published in 2000.

Professor Bloom earned his Ph.D. from Yale University in 1955 and has served on the Yale faculty since then. He is a 1985 MacArthur Foundation Award recipient, served as the Charles Eliot Norton Professor of Poetry at Harvard University in 1987–88, and has received honorary degrees from the universities of Rome and Bologna. In 1999, Professor Bloom received the prestigious American Academy of Arts and Letters Gold Medal for Criticism.

Currently, Harold Bloom is the editor of numerous Chelsea House volumes of literary criticism, including the series BLOOM'S NOTES, BLOOM'S MAJOR DRAMATISTS, BLOOM'S MAJOR NOVELISTS, MAJOR LITERARY CHARACTERS, BLOOM'S MODERN CRITICAL VIEWS, BLOOM'S MODERN CRITICAL INTERPRETATIONS, and WOMEN WRITERS OF ENGLISH AND THEIR WORKS.

Editor's Note

My Introduction mediates upon what could be called "the Shakespearean Daemonic" in Dostoevsky.

There are eight very useful Critical Views upon *Crime and Punishment* here, but particular emphasis should be given to Mikhail Bakhtin on the liminal elements in the novel, and to A. D. Nuttall on Svidrigailov.

Of the four extracts on *The Idiot*, I single out, from a strong group, Michael Holquist on "Christian" time in the book, and Elizabeth Dalton on unconscious motivations.

It is difficult to chose among the five insightful views of *Demons*. John Jones considers the affinity between Svidrigailov and Stavrogin, while René Girard explores a very different link, between Stavrogin and Prince Myshkin of *The Idiot*.

The seven extracts upon *The Brothers Karamazov* all present essential elements for understanding Dostoevsky's masterwork. They cover all the major characters, with Richard Peace on Dmitri, Robert Louis Jackson on Ivan, Valentina A. Vetlovskaya on Alyosha, and Roger B. Anderson on Father Zosima and Old Karamazov.

Introduction
HAROLD BLOOM

Dostoevsky's greatness is invested partly in his Nihilists—Raskolnikov, Svidrigailov, and Stavrogin—and partly in the Karamazovs, with their intense vitalism, inherited from their sublimely dreadful father. In my youth, I would have added Prince Myshkin, protagonist of *The Idiot,* but there is too much incoherence in the novel, and too much inconsistency in Myshkin, to sustain rereading in one's later years. *Crime and Punishment, The Demons* (or, *The Possessed*) and *The Brothers Karamazov* are Dostoevsky's major achievements in the novel. Dostoevsky always suffered from a sense of inferiority to Tolstoy, and envy is hardly hidden in his apparent praise of Tolstoy to the literary critic Strakhov:

> I see that you hold Leo Tolstoy in very high regard: I agree that here is much of *our own;* but not that much. And yet, *of all of us,* in my opinion, he has succeeded best in expressing more of what is us, and is thus worth talking about.

Quite aside from his substantial jealousy in regard to *War and Peace,* Dostoevsky implies that the Russian God is missing from Tolstoy, which is happily true. Presumably, *The Life of a Great Sinner,* Dostoevsky's projected novel, would have given full articulation to Dostoevsky's Great Russian messianism, so we can be grateful the book was never written. Dostoevsky was a pillar of Russian Orthodoxy: he believed that the Russian Christ would carry God to the rest of the world. Tolstoy, excommunicated by the Orthodox Church, hardly could be a larger contrast. The image of the father, for Dostoevsky, ideally was the Czar, representative of the Russian God. Tolstoy was his own image of the father: his severely rationalized God expressed ultimately his own horror of mortality.

Ideologically and spiritually, Dostoevsky is difficult to bear: a racist Great Russian, he hated Jews, and loathed and feared the United States, which for him was only another image of the illusory freedom he called Nihilism. When Svidrigailov, in *Crime and Punishment,* is about to commit suicide, he is accosted by a little man, whose "face had the eternal expression of resentful affliction which is so sharply etched in every Jewish face, without exception." To this Jew, Svidrigailov says that he is "going to America" and then shoots himself in the forehead.

And yet the aesthetic greatness of *Crime and Punishment* and *The Brothers Karamazov* is unquestionable. Dostoevsky the novelist transcends the idolizer of the Tsar, the anti-Semite, the enemy of human freedom. The genius of Dostoevsky pragmatically was another self, distinct from the prophet of Orthodox Russian messianism. Tolstoy was essentially similar as natural man and as the seer of *War and Peace*. Dostoevsky, unlike Tolstoy, was a great parodist: it may even be said that satiric parody is the center of Dostoevsky's art. More even than powerful satire, absolute parody is a corrosive. Something in Dostoevsky is always on the verge of parodying even his own religiosity, and his worship of authority.

The best critical account of this peculiar strength in Dostoevsky is of course Mikhail Bakhtin's, whose *Problems of Dostoevsky's Poetics* demonstrates that parody is another name for Dostoevsky's dialectical polyphony, in which opposing voices are allowed full play. Still, Bakhtin's formalistic analysis applies equally well to Dickens and to Balzac, neither of whom carries parody to the border of madness, as Dostoevsky sometimes does. Something of astonishing force can break loose in Dostoevsky, as it so frequently does in Shakespeare, whose own nihilism (as I would interpret it) was a major influence upon Dostoevsky's deep, innate nihilism, as distinct from the Russian Nihilism he parodied. The daemonic, personified by Iago in Shakespeare, transcends Dostoevsky's poetics.

A. D. Nuttall, a critic who almost always persuades me, finds a borderline schizophrenia in Raskolnikov. I would prefer the older category of the daemonic, which never ceases to sustain the protagonist until the unfortunate second chapter of the "Epilogue," where love for Sonja raises him from the dead. From start to end of the novel proper, Raskolnikov continues to believe in his Napoleonic dream of power, which reduces to the will for killing some other person, not oneself. That ought to render him dreadfully unsympathetic, but does not: the reader is seduced, despite herself, by Raskolnikov's nightmare will, by the ecstasy of trespass. Ultimately, we do not know why Raskolnikov kills, and indeed, the more he thought about it, the less Dostoevsky himself knew about it. But then, what really are Iago's motives? His direct descendant,

Milton's Satan, suffers from a Sense of Injured Merit. Iago, like Satan, has been passed over for promotion. Raskolnikov has been reduced to the status of a poor student living in a cupboard, when he ought to have been Napoleon. When he murders the two old women, then he is Napoleon, in Dostoevsky's view.

None of us wants to be Svidrigailov, or Stavrogin, or old Karamazov, but their intensity, daemonic and unconfined, seduces us also. Dostoevsky owed immediate debts to Gogol (whom he parodied) and, to a lesser degree, to Balzac and Dickens. From Shakespeare, he learned something larger, which he successfully incarnated with savage brilliance in his grand nihilists. Bakhtin remarked that in Dostoevsky "a person's every act reveals him in his totality." That seems to me even truer of Shakespeare's persons, where outward action and psychic inwardness are uncannily fused. Whatever his ideological excesses, and despite his ignoble hatreds, the artist in Dostoevsky was Shakespeare's enlightened student. ❀

Biography of Fyodor Dostoevsky

Fyodor Dostoevsky's (1821–1881) life was arguably as personally and politically harrowing as his books. Indeed, his portrait adorns the covers of some editions, and a reader might well be excused for mistaking the author for his characters—Raskolnikov in penal servitude, perhaps, or the Underground Man forever nursing his grudge.

Almost uniquely among Russia's greatest writers, Dostoevsky came not from the gentry but from Moscow's middle class. His father, a former army surgeon, had insisted that the young man become an engineer, and at 16 he obediently left for St. Petersburg to begin his training. While Fyodor was there, however, Mikhail Dostoevsky was murdered at home by his own serfs. Oedipal themes haunt many of his son's works, most obviously *Karamazov*, and Freud would later posit that Dostoevsky's epilepsy might have psychosomatic origins in a repressed wish for his father's death.

Despite being left in a poor state, Dostoevsky abandoned engineering for a far less certain future as a writer, publishing *Poor Folk*, which has been called Russia's first social novel, in 1846. The influential critic Belinsky immediately hailed him as the successor to Gogol—praise indeed for an aspiring author to whom Gogol had been a literary idol since early youth. Dostoevsky's next attempt, *The Double* (1846), was less of a critical success, but inaugurated his lifelong interest in and exploitation of the idea of the divided self. In a more sophisticated form, "Dostoevskian doubles" were to become a regular feature of his mature work.

Even as Dostoevsky continued his literary work, his political involvement deepened. A crackdown on the "Petrashevsky circle," in 1849, led to the young author being arrested for political subversion and, with twenty of his fellows, condemned to death. The sentence was commuted only after he had actually been led out before the firing squad—an experience that would resurface powerfully in *The Idiot*. That incident may also have triggered the onset of epilepsy, a disease that was to plague Dostoevsky from this period until his death, and which afflicts both Prince Myshkin and the bastard Smerdyakov.

Exiled to Siberia, where he was given only the New Testament to read, Dostoevsky underwent a profound religious and philosophical conversion. He was released from hard labor in 1854, but forced to serve in a garrison for five more years. During this time he also entered into his first marriage, an unhappy one, and completed two short works, "Uncle's Dream" and "The Village of Stepanchikovo" (both 1859).

Returning to St. Petersburg in 1859, Dostoevsky continued his literary work and founded *Time* (and, after it was shut down by the government in 1863, a successor journal called *Epoch*) with his brother Mikhail. His journalism now reflected his new, reactionary politics, and he spurned the radicals who sought to embrace the ex-political prisoner as a martyr to their cause. *The Insulted and Injured* (1861) and *The House of the Dead* (1862) were both published in *Time; Notes from the Underground*, Dostoevsky's first major work, began appearing in *Epoch* in 1864.

Nearly penniless after the bankruptcy of *Epoch* and the deaths of his wife and brother, Dostoevsky fled to Germany to try to recover his losses through gambling. (An inveterate gambler, he is said to have spent three days on end at the roulette tables after completing *The Idiot*.) Returning home in the fall of 1865, "I want to do an unprecedented and eccentric thing," he explained in a letter to a friend, "—to write thirty printed sheets within the space of four months, forming two separate novels, of which I will write one in the morning and the other in the evening . . ." He had in effect made a bet with the publisher Stellovsky, agreeing—in exchange for a much-needed advance—to either complete a manuscript by November 1866, or else forfeit to Stellovsky ownership of all his works: past, present, and to come. With the help of a young stenographer—Anna Snitkin, whom he married the following year—Dostoevsky won his bet: *The Gambler* (1867) was finished in time to cancel the debt to Stellovsky, and the "other" work completed soon after. That other work was *Crime and Punishment* (1866).

The book was an immediate success; but with creditors still at his door, Dostoevsky again left Russia, taking his young bride with him. Living in penury and still troubled by his recurrent fits, he completed *The Idiot* in 1868. This was followed by *The Eternal Husband* (1870) and—after a return home on account of illness—*Demons* (1872). Back in St. Petersburg, Dostoevsky worked as an editor for

The Citizen and also began the column *Diary of a Writer,* in which he occasionally published short works of fiction in addition to his regular journalism. He also wrote the lesser novel *A Raw Youth,* in 1875, before completing *The Brothers Karamazov* in 1880.

Yet even *Karamazov*—though his most ambitious and sweeping work—was conceived as only the beginning of the story of its hero, Alyosha. Dostoevsky lived to complete that story's first half, but died, in early 1881, before he could finish the end.

By the time of his death, Dostoevsky had achieved widespread fame in Russia; his effect on world literature of the 20th century was to be even more profound. Nietzsche acknowledged a debt to him, and he was a major influence on Kafka (who, it can be argued, was a major influence on modern writers). The unerring accuracy of his psychology of modern—and post-modern—man placed him far ahead of not only the artists but also the philosophers of his age. Dostoevsky may have explained that, too, better than anyone, when he scribbled to himself in one of his innumerable notebooks: "They call me a psychologist. It is not true. I'm only a realist." ❀

Plot Summary of
Crime and Punishment

In the Russian *Prestuplenie I Nakazanie* (*Crime and Punishment*), "nakazanie" does indeed mean punishment, but "prestuplenie" more accurately translates not as crime but as "transgression"—the "stepping-over" of the 23-year-old student, Raskolnikov. Originally intended as a first-person confession, the story was rewritten by Dostoevsky as a unique semi-detective novel—one in which the person most mystified by the crime is the man who commits it.

As the story begins, Raskolnikov is living in crushing poverty, obviously plagued by mental anguish. He goes to the apartment of the old pawnbroker, Alyona Ivanovna, who gives him only a ruble and fifteen kopecks for his father's silver watch.

Raskolnikov next stops at a tavern, there meeting Marmeladov, a drunkard whose failure—or contrarian refusal—to hold down a job has led to the forcing into prostitution of his daughter, Sonya. Marmeladov's situation is dire, but he is a comical figure; even his name is absurd. Raskolnikov helps him home and leaves the family money, but immediately regrets it.

A letter from his mother is then brought to Raskolnikov, informing him of his sister Dunya's impending marriage. Dunya, who has already barely escaped ruin by Svidrigailov, at whose house she served as governess, is clearly entering—for Raskolnikov's sake—upon a form of prostitution scarcely less degrading than Sonya's. Falling asleep in a park, Raskolnikov has a terrifying dream about himself, as a boy, watching a drunken peasant beating an old mare to death. Awakening, he asks: "God! But can it be, can it be that I will really take an axe and hit her on the head and smash her skull . . . ?" Realizing that he does not have to commit the crime, he breathes easily for the first time in days—but soon afterward learns, entirely by chance, that Alyona's half-sister Lizaveta will be absent from their apartment between six and seven on the following day.

Raskolnikov's preparations make him late. There are workmen painting the vacant apartment below; Raskolnikov mounts to Alyona's door and rings. He gives her a decoy pledge and, as she unwraps it, brings the axe down on her head. The scene that follows is one of the most haunting in all of literature—critics have referred to its "eerie phosphorescent glow"—as Raskolnikov first dispatches the old lady and then is forced to also kill the kindly Lizaveta, who is at home. He takes a wallet and a few trinkets, and manages to escape by hiding in the vacant apartment while men run to force the pawnbroker's door. He reaches his own room and passes into a stupor as **Part I** ends.

In **Part II**, a police summons arrives which the frenzied Raskolnikov at first takes to be connected to his crime. He wonders if he should confess, but the summons turns out to concern his rent. Hearing men discussing Alyona's murder, Raskolnikov faints. A man at the station-house holds "a yellow glass filled with yellow water"—a color that is to pervade the entire novel.

Raskolnikov hides the stolen things under a stone, never even stopping to count the money. He then lapses into delirium, waking to find he has been ill, cared for by his friend Razumikhin. Razumikhin's friend Zossimov comes and gossips about the murder, oblivious to Raskolnikov's agitation. Luzhin, Dunya's fiancé, suddenly arrives; they argue and Raskolnikov ultimately orders him to leave.

Raskolnikov wanders to the scene of the crime, where he alarms the workmen by asking about the blood. He then comes upon the dying Marmeladov, who has just been run over. He meets Sonya and gives Marmeladov's widow, Katerina Ivanovna, money for the funeral. At home he is greeted with joy by his mother and sister as **Part III** begins.

Raskolnikov and Razumikhin go to visit Razumikhin's uncle Porfiry, the officer investigating the old woman's murder. Porfiry asks Raskolnikov about his article, about a class of "extraordinary" people to whom the law does not apply, and also tries to trick him into admitting he had been present on the day of the crime. Returning home, Raskolnikov dreams that the old woman is laughing at him.

At Raskolnikov's rooms, in **Part IV**, Svidrigailov offers ten thousand roubles to help Dunya avoid the marriage to Luzhin. The meeting with Luzhin, at which Dunya insists Raskolnikov be present, ends with her canceling the engagement. Razumikhin, meanwhile, has fallen in love with her.

Raskolnikov pays a visit to Sonya and taunts her for her sacrifice. But Sonya's faith is firm—for her God is "everything." Raskolnikov asks her to read to him about the raising of Lazarus. He then says that on the next day, he will tell her who killed Lizaveta. The whole conversation is overheard by Svidrigailov.

Raskolnikov goes again to the station-house, where just as it becomes clear that Porfiry has been suspecting him, the painter Mikolka appears and admits to the murder.

In **Part V**—after a failed attempt by Luzhin to frame Sonya for theft—Raskolnikov confesses his crime to her. "What, what have you done to yourself?" she cries. She asks if he had wanted the money to care for his mother. But Raskolnikov admits that he could have worked, like Razumikhin, but "turned spiteful," wanting to know "Would I be able to step over, or not!" Sonya is about to exchange crosses with him, as a symbol of how they will bear the cross together, but he suddenly tells her to wait.

A delirious Katerina Ivanovna is now brought to Sonya's room. Svidrigailov promises to settle a sum of money on the orphans, and also makes clear to Raskolnikov that he heard the confession to Sonya.

In **Part VI**, Porfiry finally admits to knowing Raskolnikov is guilty—"Who killed them? . . . But *you* did, Rodion Romanych! You killed them, sir . . . "—but does not arrest him; Raskolnikov needs, he explains, to confess to the crime himself. Raskolnikov will henceforth waver between Svidrigailov, to whose amoralism he is insensibly drawn, and the piety of Sonya. Svidrigailov tells Dunya about her brother's guilt, offering to save him if she will yield to him. She suddenly produces a gun and fires at him twice, but misses. At last she throws the gun away; but when he realizes she will never love him, he lets her go. After wandering the city he presents himself before a sentry, announces that he is "going to America," and shoots himself. As Donald Fanger notes, "the purity of comic effect is preserved by closing the scene with the pulling of the trigger: we do not hear the shot or see the body fall; his death is no more meaningful or real than his life; he can, as it were, vanish but not die."

Raskolnikov finally goes to the police to confess. Again hesitating, he is about to leave but sees Sonya and, turning back into the station-house, declares: "*It was I who killed the official's old widow and her sister Lizaveta with an axe and robbed them . . .*"

Critical consensus has broadly been against the **Epilogue,** which attempts to compress a full year into a few pages, though the novel proper spans mere days. Raskolnikov is sentenced to only eight years, because he was mentally unbalanced at the time of the murder; because (we now learn) he had previously performed a number of good deeds; and because he confessed. Though Sonya looks after him faithfully, Raskolnikov continues to refuse true repentance. But, at last, he embraces her and weeps: "They were resurrected by love." ❦

List of Characters in
Crime and Punishment

Raskolnikov is an impoverished student who is the central character of the novel. He divides humanity into the "ordinary," those who must live in submission and are required to obey the law, and the "extraordinary," those who are above the law. To prove that he is among the "extraordinary," Raskolnikov commits a brutal crime—the murder of a pawnbroker and her gentle stepsister. Consumed by guilt but still believing he is above the law, he agonizes over confessing to the crime. When he finally confesses, he is sentenced to seven years in prison. There he is redeemed by the acceptance of his fate and the healing power of Sonya's love.

Marmeladov is a drunkard whom Raskolnikov meets in a bar. Even though his drinking impoverishes his family and forces his daughter Sonya into prostitution, Marmeladov is an absurdly comic figure. He meets his end by being run over by a carriage.

Katerina Ivanovna is Marmeladov's pitiable wife. She was widowed with three children before marrying the irresponsible Marmeladov. She is the persuasive force behind Sonya's entrance into the underworld of prostitution. She later dies in Sonya's room.

Sonya is Marmeladov's eldest daughter who has been forced into prostitution to support her family. Despite the suffering she endures, her religious faith remains unwavering. When she falls in love with Raskolnikov, she pledges to take up his cross with him and follows him to prison. There, her steadfast love becomes the instrument of his redemption.

Pulcheria Alexandrovna is Raskolnikov's mother. Though timid, she has made great sacrifices to pay for Raskolnikov's education. Even as her family falls on hard times, she carries herself with dignity and is intensely devoted to her two children.

Dunya is Raskolnikov's strong-willed sister. Beautiful and intelligent, she agrees to marry the rich but overbearing Luzhin to ease her family's poverty. She remains loyal to Raskolnikov even after she finds out he is the murderer. When Luzhin tries to bully her and her mother into renouncing Raskolnikov, she breaks off the engagement.

Razumikhin is Raskolnikov's most dependable friend. When Raskolnikov confesses, he entrusts Razumikhin with taking care of his mother and sister. Razumikhin eventually falls in love with and marries Dunya.

Luzhin is Dunya's vain and pompous fiancé who wants to marry someone poor so she will be beholden to him. He attempts to discredit Raskolnikov and is forced to leave when his plan backfires.

Svidrigailov is Dunya's lecherous former employer who tries to seduce her. He commits suicide when he realizes that she will never love him.

Porfiry Petrovich is the clever police detective working on the pawnbroker's and her half-sister's murder cases. Although he knows Raskolnikov is guilty, he instead pressures him to confess and confront his crime. ❋

Critical Views on
Crime and Punishment

GEORGE GIBIAN ON SYMBOLISM AND THE EPILOGUE

[George Gibian (1924–1999) was Goldwin Smith Professor of Russian Literature at Cornell University and author of *Tolstoj and Shakespeare* (1957) and *Interval of Freedom: Soviet Literature During the Thaw, 1954–1957* (1960). Here, he examines the use of Christian and pagan symbols throughout the novel and especially in the epilogue, where the indirect, non-verbal nature of their message mirrors the step Raskolnikov himself must take—beyond rationalism and dialectic—in order to be redeemed.]

External evidence of Dostoevsky's bent to think of the action in terms of its Christian archetypes exists in Dostoevsky's notebook. On the same page we find the following somewhat enigmatic entries:

> When she is persuading him, i.e. before the farewell.
> Well kiss the gospel, kiss it, read it.
>
> Lazarus, arise.
>
> And then when Svidrigaylov gives her money.
> I myself was dead Lazarus, and Christ raised me from the dead.
>
> NB Sonya follows him to Golgotha, forty paces behind.[11]
> ⟨...⟩

The notebook proves that Dostoevsky thought of the pervasive biblical references as a connected series which was to be noticed; the individual parallels, scattered as they are in the final version of the novel, are to be thought of together, as a steady accompaniment to the story of Raskolnikov, an underpinning of allusions to Christ's and Lazarus' deaths and rebirths.

The Christian symbolism is underlined by the pagan and universal symbolism of the earth. Sonya persuades Raskolnikov not only to confess and wear the cross, but also to kiss the earth at the crossroads—a distinctly Russian and pre-Christian acknowledgment of the earth as the common mother of all men.[12] The earth is the source of fertility and the sanction for all family and community ties. It is fitting to confess to the earth: "Go at once, this very minute, and stand at the crossroads, bow down, first kiss the earth which you have defiled, and then bow down to the whole world, to all four sides—and then say to all men aloud, I am a murderer! Then God will send you life again" (p. 433). In bowing to the earth and kissing it, Raskolnikov is performing a symbolic and non-rational act; the rationalist is marking the beginning of his change into a complete, organic, living human being, rejoining all other men in the community. ⟨...⟩

⟨...⟩ Sonya plays in the novel a part comparable to that performed by Beatrice and Lucia taken jointly in the *Divine Comedy*. Her name is a clue, as so often happens with Dostoevsky's emphatically significant names. Sonya stands for Sophia, which in Russian thought occupies a position far more important than merely that of its literal meaning, wisdom. ⟨...⟩

It was Sonya who had brought Raskolnikov the message of Lazarus and his resurrection; she had given him the cypress cross and urged him to kiss the earth at the crossroads. On the evening of the day when, by the bank of the river and in the presence of Sonya, Raskolnikov's regeneration had begun, the New Testament lies under his pillow as a reminder of the Christian prototype of resurrection which had been stressed earlier in the novel. Against the background of all the important symbols of the book, Easter, spring, Abraham's flocks, the earth of Siberia, the river, the dream, and Sonya, the drama within Raskolnikov's mind assumes its expressive outward form.

There follow several explicit statements of what happened. We read that "the dawn of a full resurrection to a new life" was already shining "in their faces, that love brought them back to life, that the heart of one held inexhaustible sources of life for the heart of the other," and that "the gradual rebirth" of Raskolnikov would follow (pp. 557–559). But the power of the general, overt statements depends on the indirect, oblique, dramatic, and symbolic statements which preceded them and prepared the ground for our acceptance of them. ⟨...⟩

Notes

[11] Glivenko, *Iz arkhiva F. M. Dostoevskogo: Prestuplenic i nakazanie* (Moscow-Leningrad, 1931), p. 204. There are further references to Christ on pp. 73, 76, and 177.

[12] The importance of Mother Earth in Russian thought has been frequently discussed. See esp. R. V. Pletnyov, "Zemlja," in A. L. Bem, ed. *O Dostoevkom: sbornik statey* (Prague, 1929), I, 153–162; Zander, *Dostoevsky*, pp. 36–65; and Georgy Fedotov, *Stikhi dukhovnye* (Paris, 1935), passim. My article "Dostoevsky's Use of Russian Folklore," forthcoming in the *Journal of American Folklore*, deals with the relationship between folk literature and Dostoevsky's works in general, including the theme of Mother Earth.

—George Gibian, "Traditional Symbolism in *Crime and Punishment*," *Publications of the Modern Language Association of America* LXX, no. 5 (1955): pp. 990–91, 994–95.

Edward Wasiolek on the Plot

[Edward Wasiolek is Distinguished Service Professor Emeritus of Russian, English, and Comparative Literature at the University of Chicago. His books include *Crime and Punishment and the Critics* (1961), *Dostoevsky: The Major Fiction* (1964), and *Tolstoy's Major Fiction* (1978), and he edited the notebooks to all four major novels. In this extract, Wasiolek challenges the prevailing view of *Crime and Punishment* as casually or haphazardly plotted by showing that "the character, action, and image of the first half emerge antithetically in the second half."]

⟨T⟩he extreme antitheses that mark the course of Raskolnikov's internal fortunes are coextensive throughout. He is both rational and irrational, proud and humble throughout; but one set of principles is dominant in the first half of the novel, the other in the second half. In both halves of the novel the less dominant set bursts erratically through the dominating set. Raskolnikov, for example, though characterized in the first half of the novel by isolation, pride, and even hate, acts at times unpredictably—when he pities the young streetwalker, helps the Marmeladov family, and reacts with despair to the dream of the brutal beating of a mare—according to impulses of the opposite kind. Similarly, in the second half, though he is moved to repentance and confession and, by his love for Sonia, to communion with his fellow men, he rebels against these impulses, especially in the epilogue, with the fury of the self-willed character of the first half. The structure of *Crime and Punishment* must therefore be modified from a linear antithetical balance to one of two sets of antitheses that cross at the middle somewhat in the fashion of a flattened X. One line of dominant motives fades and another, antithetical in character, rises into dominance. But neither disappears: from beginning to end Raskolnikov carries both within him. ⟨...⟩

Since Sonia and Svidrigaylov will objectify Raskolnikov's conflicting impulses in the second half of the novel, and since we can expect the incidents, images, and physical details to be informed by the structure as described, we should find in the second half two focal points analogous in importance to that of the murder in the first half, one opposite and one similar, but more desperate, in character. We should, in effect, expect two visits, two testings, one negating the first, the other prolonging into desperation the first. Let us consider first the analogous scene opposite in character: whereas the first scene was one of death, this should be one of rebirth; whereas the first is built on a rational and self-willed principle, this should be built on an irrational and will-less principle. This is precisely what we find. Sonia, the symbol of true rebirth in faith, balances antithetically the image of the murdered Alyona Ivanovna, the symbol of false rebirth. Raskolnikov now visits Sonia instead of Alyona, and instead of death, there is birth in the reading of the story of Lazarus.[13] And if the murder is the central point of the testing of the rational principle, the confession becomes the central point of the testing of Raskolnikov's rebirth. Appropriately, since these two scenes balance each other, there is a rehearsal for the confession as there was for the murder scene.

But Sonia, in the second half of the novel, as the explicit and fully developed antithesis to Alyona, should be anticipated in the first half of the novel, according to the structure as defined above, by a less developed, less explicit antithesis and one to which Raskolnikov is less fully and more fitfully sympathetic. Such a need is met by Marmeladov's role in the story and specifically and vividly by the image of blood that links Raskolnikov antithetically with the murdered Alyona and Marmeladov. On two occasions Raskolnikov was splattered with blood: in killing Alyona and in carrying the dying body of Marmeladov. For Raskolnikov the blood is first a sign of death, then of life.

Note
[13] Dostoevski's desire to balance the picture of false rebirth against that of true rebirth is even clearer in his notebooks, where he originally planned to have Raskolnikov see a vision of Christ (*Iz Arkhiva*, p. 70).

—Edward Wasiolek, "On the Structure of *Crime and Punishment*," *Publications of the Modern Language Association of America* LXXIV, no. 1 (1959): pp. 132–34.

W. D. Snodgrass on the Women and the Mare

[W. D. Snodgrass (b. 1926) is a Pulitzer laureate, a Fellow of the Academy of American Poets, and the author of *Heart's Needle* (1959), *After Experience* (1968), and *The Führer Bunker* (1995). In this landmark essay, he examines Raskolnikov's relationships with the various women of the novel—the girl on the boulevard, Dunya, Sonya, Katerina Ivanovna, Pulcheria Alexandrovna, and finally the pawnbroker—and considers their significance in Raskolnikov's dream of the beating of the mare.]

⟨. . .⟩ Marmeladov's wife makes openly the accusations which Raskolnikov's mother only implies. (This does not make the accusation less threatening; when only implied, it is much harder to answer.) Seeing Marmeladov beaten by his wife, Raskolnikov must have imagined himself—and to some extent wished himself—beaten by his mother. Yet this letter from the mother makes plain a stronger and even more frightening resemblance of the mother, Pulcheria Alexandrovna, to the landlady, Pashenka, and so finally to the pawnbroker, Alyona Ivanovna. For if Raskolnikov has intentionally picked Alyona Ivanovna to stand in the image of Pashenka, he has picked both to stand in the image of his mother. They form a triumvirate of older women, each accompanied by a younger woman, each a widow. From each Raskolnikov has asked and received something; to each he is indebted. They hold his spirit as a pledge. They seem to him tormentors, since it is on their account that he torments himself. When Raskolnikov strikes down the pawnbroker with an axe, he will strike at Pashenka; but he will also strike behind her at the image of his greatest creditor, his mother. Good reason then that, later in the book, when he is ready to face the police and confess to murdering the pawnbroker, meeting instead his mother, still alive and ready to accuse him not only for his past failures, but for this new stroke against her as well, he will fall in a dead faint. Good reason, too that when he recovers and she offers to sit up beside him that night, he cries, "Don't torture me!" 〈...〉

〈W〉here is Raskolnikov in his dream? Is he the horse, the little boy, the father, or the brute Mikolka? The answer must be Yes. All of the characters of the dream are the dreamer. The problem is not to decide who is who, but rather to understand the tenor of the dreamer's apprehension of the world, that is, of his mind.

That is not so difficult as it might seem. The dream shows Raskolnikov to himself as a man too feeble in drawing his burdens, yet entirely too strong in punishing himself for that failure. Thus he is stuck on a treadmill of guilt and rage where he is beating himself to death for being stuck. At the same time, the dream shows him a world which has the same characteristics: all good characters are weak or victimized. (The dream contains but disguises the fact that these characters have chosen to be either weak or victimized.) Meantime, "the worst are full of passionate intensity." The only active role in the dream belongs to such destroyers as Mikolka. Raskolnikov's dream tells him that he must choose either murder or suicide; either kill or be killed.

For the horse, also, I have given what must seem disparate interpretations. Does the horse represent the teen-aged girl, Dunya and Sonia, Or does it represent the pawnbroker, the landlady and the mother, Or Marmeladov and Raskolnikov? Once again, the answer to all the questions is Yes. To miss the identity of all these characters as symbolized by the horse is to miss an essential texture of Raskolnikov's mind. In particular, we must recognize the identity of Raskolnikov with the pawnbroker he kills. I have already pointed out that he has picked Alyona Ivanovna as exemplifying the worst qualities of his mother—debt collecting and tyranny. Again, I have shown that Raskolnikov shares many of those worst qualities (no doubt his mother was an effective teacher)—especially the technique of intentional mismanagement so as to blame others and collect debts against them. These are the very qualities he wants to punish in himself and so to annihilate. Thus, he has chosen Alyona Ivanovna to stand not only as a scapegoat for his mother, but much more important, for himself. ⟨...⟩

The fact that Raskolnikov wakes with the assumption that the dream meant murder:

> Good God! ... is it possible that I will really take a hatchet, hit her on the head. ...

instead of the only other alternative, suicide, indicates what choice he has made.

—W. D. Snodgrass, "Crime for Punishment: The Tenor of Part One," *The Hudson Review* XIII, no. 2 (1960): pp. 219–20, 239–40.

Pierre R. Hart on the Narrator

[Pierre R. Hart was Assistant Professor of Russian at the State University of New York at Buffalo and author of *G. R. Derzhavin: A Poet's Progress* (1978). In this extract, he examines the "combination of omniscient description and 'narrated monologue'" used by Dostoevsky's narrator, and its special role in a novel that had originally been planned as a first-person "confession."]

⟨...⟩ Within those scenes where Raskol'nikov's impressions are primary, there is a tendency to move from the mere report of the protagonist's observations to a more dramatic form which incorporates some of the features of colloquial speech. As the narration shifts between these modes, the identities of the narrator and Raskol'nikov tend to merge, producing a category of statements that might ultimately be attributed to either of them.⁹ In defining the narrator's function, then, we must take into account both the source of a remark and the possible modifications it has undergone in the process of transmission.

One of the narrator's primary functions is to provide information about Raskol'nikov which the hero is either unable or unwilling to admit to himself. As he makes the final arguments for and against his plan to murder, the reader is provided with an independent commentary on the hero's condition. Throughout the novel, Raskol'nikov will return to the question of whether he is in full possession of his senses. Seen from the narrator's standpoint, the issue is resolved from the outset: "It would have been difficult to sink to a lower ebb of disorder..." and further "This is what happens to *some monomaniacs* [emphasis mine] who are excessively concentrated on one thing."[10] ⟨...⟩

Since salvation can only be attained through personal acknowledgement of error, the narrator must endure the agonizingly slow progress which his hero makes, without hope of changing its tempo or direction. Obviously unproductive repetitions in Raskol'nikov's thought and behavior elicit expressions of somewhat impatient concern. Everything which might be offered as a justification for the crime must be evaluated against the store of previous experience. As Raskol'nikov makes one of his first attempts to understand the true motivation for his crime, he is struck by the curious fact that he failed to take the money from the pawnbroker's purse. His immediate reaction is to dismiss this as an oversight due to illness. The narrator's intrusion at this point serves to remind us that the question cannot be so readily resolved: "Yes, that's so, that's all so: But he had known that before and it was not at all a new question for him." (116) To recognize that this is an old question is to place the validity of economic motivation in doubt, something which Raskol'nikov is not yet fully prepared to do. Thus, the narrator can counter Raskol'nikov's arguments rhetorically, but it still remains for the latter to work through the welter of apparent motivations independently.

With regard to external events and objects, the narrator assumes a somewhat different function, providing supplementary detail which is quite compatible with that offered by Raskol'nikov directly. In fact, the initial portrayal of Lužin depends largely upon the narrator's commentary and it is only subsequently that Raskol'nikov makes his own scorn for this figure completely evident. ⟨...⟩

The parenthetic remark may also be used to establish one of several moods in the course of a conversation. During Raskol'nikov's second visit to Sonja, he attempts to rationalize the motivation for his crime. Before he can complete his explanation, the narrator interjects: "(He spoke as though he had learned it in advance.)" (434) The immediate implication is that Raskol'nikov no longer has faith in his ideas nor does he really expect Sonja to believe him. The speech becomes a sort of involuntary purge rather than a sincere confession and, in a second parenthetic remark, the narrator offers a possible explanation for this unexpected garrulousness: "(Really, he had been too long without talking with anyone!)"(436) ⟨...⟩

⟨The narrator⟩ is the inventory keeper for Raskol'nikov's experience and calls attention to the errors, repetitions, and ill-advised judgments that he makes. Through his active role as commentator, he provides a point of reference external to Raskol'nikov, with which his hero's perception of the world can be compared. While Raskol'nikov's story is unquestionably the focal point of the novel, his perception of the story is not. By maintaining his perceptual initiative, the narrator prevents the novel from becoming a clinical study in psychology.

Notes

[9] Zundelovič, p. 14, goes so far as to state: "It's as though the author were transformed into his hero and they were speaking in unison."

[10] F. M. Dostoevskij, *Sobranie sočinenij* (Moscow, 1957), V, 32. All subsequent quotations from *Crime and Punishment* are taken from this edition. Numbers in parentheses following quotations indicate the appropriate pages.

—Pierre R. Hart, "Looking Over Raskol'nikov's Shoulder: The Narrator in 'Crime and Punishment,'" *Criticism* XIII, no. 2 (1971): pp. 169, 171, 178, 179.

W. WOODIN ROWE ON ANTINOMY

[W. Woodin Rowe has taught at George Washington University and is the author of *Nabokov's Deceptive World* (1971), *Through Gogol's Looking Glass: Reverse Vision, False Focus, and Precarious Logic* (1976), and *Nabokov and Others: Patterns in Russian Literature* (1979). Below, he shows how Dostoevsky uses narrative antinomy—by first making an assertion, then contradicting it, and finally implying that both are somewhat true—to give the reader an unnerving sense of being at one with Raskolnikov's thoughts.]

⟨...⟩ Dostoevskij creates antinomic effects by means of a three-stage formulation which may be likened to the swinging of a pendulum from one side to the other and then at least partially back. This final swing tends to reconcile the two extremes, and Dostoevskij's reader is led to accept a (muted) contradiction. ⟨...⟩

As the novel opens, we are told that Raskol'nikov always experienced "some kind of sickly and cowardly sensation" while passing his landlady's door on the stairs. He was heavily in debt to her and was afraid of meeting her. "Not that he was so cowardly or downtrodden, quite the contrary; but for some time now he had been in a tense and irritable condition resembling hypochondria." Raskol'nikov's sickly cowardice is denied; its opposite affirmed. His state of nervousness and near hypochondria then tends to reconcile the two extremes. The reader may even sense here Raskol'nikov's mental attempt to justify his own apparent cowardice. This effect soon becomes more obvious: "Actually, he was not afraid of any landlady at all, no matter what this one happened to be plotting against him. But to stop on the stairs and listen to all sorts of nonsense about all those commonplace, trivial things...." By this time the reader has been subtly introduced to Raskol'nikov's inner feelings through his own point of view. ⟨...⟩

Porfirij tells Raskol'nikov to submit a short statement about his pawned belongings. "On ordinary paper?" Raskol'nikov inquires. "'Oh, as ordinary as can be!' and suddenly Porfirij Petrovič looked at him with a kind of obvious mockery, screwing up his eyes as if winking at him. This however may only have seemed so to Raskol'nikov, because it lasted only a moment. At least there had been something like that. Raskol'nikov could have sworn he had winked at him, the devil only knew why. 'He knows!' flashed through him like lightning." Here, both reader and Raskol'nikov are led to believe that Porfirij (1) seemed to wink, (2) may not have, and (3) probably did. Our haunting suspicion that he definitely did wink, however, is doubly intensified since Raskol'nikov wonders why he winked and even deduces from the wink that Porfirij knows of his crime. Porfirij later asks Raskol'nikov if he himself, according to his theory, might be able to go beyond the law: "'Oh, for instance, kill and steal?' And once again he somehow suddenly winked at him with his left eye, laughing inaudibly—just exactly as he had before." This implicit reaffirmation of our previous suspicion (that Porfirij did wink) subtly re-establishes the reader's position inside Raskol'nikov's mind at a key point in the encounter. ⟨...⟩

After he finally arrives to admit his guilt, Raskol'nikov suddenly leaves, only to return and confess. This three-stage action may be seen to preview a final protracted patterning, of which it is but the first step. The second step occurs in the Epilogue, where the killer still seems, in A. L. Bem's phrase, "under the spell" of his theory. "Only in this sense did he acknowledge his crime: merely that he had not carried it through, and had turned himself in and confessed." At another point he even decides: "My conscience is clear." The last scene, however, where we read that "love resurrected" Raskol'nikov and Sonja, completes a final patterning by reaffirming the idea of confession, symbolized by the fact that Raskol'nikov opens the Gospel, "the very one from which she had read to him about the resurrection of Lazarus." Yet the effect is typically blurred and perhaps even purposely unconvincing. That is, we sense a familiar tension in this closing sequence of confession, denial, and precipitous reaffirmation. By virtue of patterned antinomy, our final impression is rather that Raskol'nikov has still not fully repented, yet he seems at last at to be irrevocably headed in this direction.

—W. Woodin Rowe, "Dostoevskian Patterned Antinomy and Its Function in *Crime and Punishment*," *Slavic and East European Journal* XVI, no. 3 (1972): pp. 287, 288, 289–90, 292.

Mikhail Bakhtin on Carnival

[Mikhail Bakhtin's (1895–1975) books include *Rabelais and His World* (1968), *Problems in Dostoevsky's Poetics* (1973), *The Formal Method in Literary Scholarship: A Critical Introduction to Sociological Poetics* (with P. N. Medvedev, 1978), and *The Dialogic Imagination: Four Essays* (1981). In this extract, he considers the role of "carnival" in Dostoevsky, showing how "Everything in this novel—people's fates, their experiences and ideas—approaches its own borders, everything is, as it were, prepared to become its own opposite... everything is taken to the extreme, to its limit."]

It is characteristic that the very setting of the novel's action—*Petersburg* (its role in the novel is enormous)—is on the border of existence and nonexistence, of reality and a phantasmagoria which is about to dissipate and vanish like a fog. Petersburg too is seemingly devoid of inner grounds for a justified stabilization; it too is on the threshold. ⟨...⟩

In Raskolnikov's dream it is not only the murdered old woman (actually she is not murdered in the dream, since it turns out to be impossible to kill her) who laughs, but also people somewhere else, in the bedroom, who constantly laugh louder and louder. Then a crowd appears, a multitude of people, both on the *stairway* and *below;* in relation to this crowd passing below him, Raskolnikov is located *at the head of the stairs.* We have before us the image of a carnival impostor-king being subjected to the discrowning ridicule of the entire folk on the public square. The square is a symbol of belonging to the whole folk (*vsenarodnost'*), and at the end of the novel Raskolnikov, before giving himself up at the police station, appears on the square and bows deep down to the earth before the folk (*narod*). ⟨...⟩

⟨...⟩ Dostoevsky almost never makes use of the interior space of houses or rooms, far from his borders, i.e. far from the threshold, except, of course, for scandalous scenes and discrownings, when interior space (the drawing room or the hall) becomes a substitute for the square. Dostoevsky "leaps over" all that is homey and settled and stable and far from the threshold, the inner space of houses, apartments and rooms, because the life which he depicts is not played out in that kind of space. Dostoevsky was least of all an estate-domestic-room-apartment-family writer. In homey interior space, far from the threshold, people live a biographical life in biographical time: they are born, they experience childhood and youth, enter into marriage, give birth to children, grow old, and die. And Dostoevsky "leaps over" that kind of biographical time, too. On the threshold and on the square the only possible time is *crisis time,* in which the *instant* is equal to years, decades, even to "a billion years." ⟨...⟩

⟨. . .⟩ Raskolnikov lives in essence on the *threshold:* his narrow room, "the coffin" (here a carnival symbol), opens directly onto the *stairway landing,* and he never locks his door, even when he goes out (i.e. his room is unenclosed inner space). In this "coffin" it is impossible to live a biographical life—in it one can only experience a crisis, make an ultimate decision, die or be born anew (as in the graves in "Bobok" or in the "ridiculous man's" coffin). Marmeladov's family also lives on the threshold, in a walk-through room (*proxodnaia komnata*) which opens directly onto a stairway (there, on the threshold, Raskol'nikov meets the members of the family for the first time when he brings the drunken Marmeladov home). He experiences terrifying moments on the threshold of the old usuress whom he has murdered, when the people who have come to visit her are standing on the other side of the door, on the stairway landing, ringing the bell. He comes again to this place and rings the bell himself, in order to experience these moments anew. The scene of his half-confession to Razumikhin, expressed only by glances, without words, takes place on the threshold in the corridor by a lamp. His conversations with Sonya take place on the threshold, near the door leading to the neighboring apartment (with Svidrigailov eavesdropping on the other side). It goes without saying that there is no need to enumerate all of the "*performances*" ("*deistva*") which take place in this novel on or near the threshold, or which exude the living sensation of the threshold.

—Mikhail Bakhtin, *Problems of Dostoevsky's Poetics,* R. W. Rotsel, trans. (Ann Arbor: Ardis, 1973): pp. 140–42.

W. J. LEATHERBARROW ON PORFIRY

[W. J. Leatherbarrow is Professor of Russian and Slavonic Studies at the University of Sheffield. He is the author of *Fedor Dostoevsky* (1981) and *Fyodor Dostoyevsky: The Brothers Karamazov* (1992), and editor of *A Documentary History of Russian Thought: From the Enlightenment to Marxism* (1987) and *Dostoevskii and Britain* (1995). Below, he demonstrates how Porfiry functions as one of

Raskolnikov's many "doubles"—specifically, as the external projection of his desire for punishment.]

Porfirii is aligned with Raskolnikov in the reader's mind from the time when Razumikhin first mentions him:

> Porfirii also wants to make your acquaintance.

From this deceptively innocent first mention Porfirii grows in Raskolnikov's subconscious until eventually he is identified precisely with the latter's need for arrest and punishment. ⟨...⟩

In his interpretation of Porfirii's "wink" Raskolnikov is beginning to allow his imagination to manipulate Porfirii into acting and speaking as his urge to be punished would wish the detective to behave. At times from this point onwards the conversation with Porfirii seems uncannily like a monologue in which Raskolnikov presents and discusses his own doubts about his behaviour in killing the old woman. ⟨...⟩

Occasionally, the real Porfirii breaks through the one existing only in Raskolnikov's imagination. For example, when Raskolnikov, convinced that Porfirii knows all, loses his self-control and admits recognition of Porfirii's suspicions, a totally new detective emerges, one who is not only genuinely concerned and upset, but who also seems to believe that Raskolnikov is innocent and suffering from a persecution complex. ⟨...⟩

The final interview is handled magnificently. In it Raskolnikov creates and recreates a Porfirii who will satisfy all the demands of his urge to be arrested. By this stage Porfirii has lost almost all semblance of reality; like a ghost he visits Raskolnikov who is alone in the room where the murder was conceived and planned, and, like a ghost, he leaves after the interview and disappears, never to appear again during the course of the novel. ⟨...⟩

Immediately prior to Porfirii's "visit" Raskolnikov has heard of the confession of Mikolka, and has been told by Razumikhin that Porfirii is apparently convinced by this confession. ⟨...⟩ Porfirii's chase ended, Raskolnikov's need for punishments reasserts itself:

> Raskolnikov felt the rush of a new kind of fright. The thought that Porfirii considered him innocent suddenly began to alarm him.

So, quite suddenly, following Raskolnikov's new state of mind, his fear of being thought innocent, Porfirii begins to change. His monologue after Raskolnikov's "rush of fright" is very different from the apologetic tone of what he has hitherto said. He returns to a detailed examination of Raskolnikov's behaviour throughout the affair. With remarkable perception he isolates the motive behind every step taken by Raskolnikov, from the conception of the idea and the writing of the article to his behaviour when confronted with an accusation of murder from an unknown artisan. Raskol'nikov is thrown into confusion by this detective "who has seen through him, but has now gone back upon himself". He now realises that the only thing standing in the way of Porfirii's suspecting him is Mikolka and his confession. Accordingly, in the next part of Porfirii's explanation, Raskolnikov, driven by his urge to suffer punishment, has *Mikolka disappear.* More precisely, he diverts Porfirii's suspicions from Mikolka to himself by having Porfirii's conception of Mikolka turn into a "shadowy double" of himself. This begins when Porfirii reveals that Mikolka is an Old Believer; the significance of this point is missed in English, but the original Russian reveals all: "*on iz raskol'nikov*". ⟨...⟩

The schismatic's behaviour in deliberately inviting suffering is matched by Raskolnikov's killing in order to humiliate himself and by his inviting suspicion from Zamyotov and others. The original image of Mikolka is in this way blurred beyond recognition and is replaced by an image of Raskolnikov himself—an image which is indistinct, but recognisable nonetheless. The final barrier between Raskolnikov and his desired goal, discovery, is broken down, and Porfirii's next comment is:

> Why, *you* are the murderer, Rodion Romanych! You are the murderer, sir. . . .

—W. J. Leatherbarrow, "Raskolnikov and the 'Enigma of his Personality,'" *Forum for Modern Language Studies* IX, no. 2 (1973): pp. 160–64.

A. D. Nuttall on Svidrigailov

[A. D. Nuttall is Professor of English and a Fellow of New College, Oxford. His books include *Two Concepts of Allegory: A Study of Shakespeare's* Tempest *and the Logic of Allegorical Expression* (1967), *A Common Sky: Philosophy and the Literary Imagination* (1974), and *A New Mimesis* (1983). Here he shows that, had Dostoevsky intended his novel to be unambiguously Christian, he would not have given us Svidrigailov—who, though a Christian failure, is an existential success.]

⟨. . .⟩ Svidrigailov the murderer and rapist is never as frightening as Svidrigailov the watcher and listener. To learn that the whole of Raskolnikov's confession to Sonia was overheard by Svidrigailov is at once disgusting and alarming. For a literary precedent one must turn to *Les Liaisons Dangèreuses,* or even to *Othello.* Our modern term for that which engages the mind in a wholly neutral fashion—"interesting"—is absent from Shakespeare's vocabulary, but if it had been present, Iago would have used it. Svidrigailov's reaction to what he hears pass between Raskolnikov and Sonia is very Iago-like:

> But all that time Mr Svidrigailov had been standing listening at the door of the empty room . . . The conversation had struck him as interesting and remarkable.

Svidrigailov lives the life implied by Raskolnikov's most fundamental theory. He oversteps, innovates, moves in any direction. His life is the endless utterance of a new language. One is tempted to say that he is the better existentialist of the two but the word "existentialist" implies the intellectual acceptance of a theory, and Svidrigailov derives much of his power from the fact that he is unfettered by theory. We have already seen in the Underground Man how this particular sort of existentialism is essentially self-destructive. The theory proposes a pure spontaneity, but no one can be purely spontaneous who acts to demonstrate a theory. Raskolnikov in soliloquy desperately acknowledges that he cannot attain transcendent freedom, that he is, after all, no better than a louse: ". . . what shows that I am utterly a louse is that . . . *I felt beforehand* that I should tell myself so *after* killing her . . . The vulgarity! The abjectness!" Raskolnikov is trapped in his own endlessly rationalising consciousness. All the time, both in prospect and retrospect, he is *constructing* his own life as a story, and the whole point about the freedom he desires is that it must not be constructed in this way. Svidrigailov is free from this itch. He is not constantly saying to himself and to others, "Look how unpredictable I am." He lives without casuistry. ⟨. . .⟩

But if Svidrigailov is as we have described him, what has happened to our picture of *Crime and Punishment* as showing the essential servitude of existential freedom? If we had only Raskolnikov to deal with, that position would be secure. But with the smiling figure of Svidrigailov watching us from the shadows as we watched Raskolnikov in the novel, a different hypothesis presents itself. Raskolnikov reverted to Christian values, not because the other path is intrinsically impassable, but simply because he, personally, lacked the strength to follow it. Doubtless his final submission shows more virtue, more goodness than his rebellion, but then virtue of that kind was never required of the existential hero. The implication is clear: Raskolnikov is an existential failure, and we know this because, stalking behind him through the novel is the living embodiment of existential success. ⟨. . .⟩

If the lesson of the Raskolnikov spatial imagery is that his crime was the quintessence of un-freedom, what by parity of reasoning are we to make of the suicide of Svidrigailov? The Christian interpretation of *Crime and Punishment,* as we have seen, really needs here a similar bias in the narrative technique. But instead we are given water, space and air. ⟨. . .⟩

⟨. . .⟩ I do not argue that the wind and weather that attend on Svidrigailov's death are uniformly delightful. Manifestly, they carry both relief and terror. I claim only a fundamental antithesis. Heat, confinement and suffocation are one thing; wind, rain and morning mist are another. If the former mean the denial of freedom, the latter must, by the language of images we have learned, mean freedom; freedom with all its horror, but the real thing. We may say of Svidrigailov what was once said of another inhabitant of Hell:

> . . . *E parve di costoro*
> *Quegli che vince e non colui che perde.*

—A. D. Nuttall, *Crime and Punishment: Murder as Philosophic Experiment* (Edinburgh: Sussex University Press, 1978): pp. 57–58, 59, 62, 65.

Plot Summary of
The Idiot

Dostoevsky originally intended in Myshkin the portrayal of a "positively good" human being, and the prince's childlike qualities are indeed apparent from the moment we meet him aboard a train bound for St. Petersburg. With him are Lebedyev, a minor official, and Rogozhin, a wealthy young man. Myshkin has been in treatment for epilepsy in Switzerland; now, with little more than the clothes on his back, he is going to seek out his only surviving relative, the wife of General Yepanchin.

At the Yepanchins', Myshkin throws the footman into confusion by engaging him in a discussion of capital punishment. After meeting the general, the prince is struck by a photograph of Nastasya Filippovna, and we are told her history.

Upon the death of her father, Nastasya had been adopted by her neighbor Totsky; he spent a considerable sum on her education and, at sixteen, seduced her. Totsky has now resolved to settle down with Alexandra Yepanchin, but though he and Nastasya are no longer involved, she has frustrated all his previous attempts to marry. Totsky is frankly afraid of Nastasya—as well he might be—and his new scheme is to marry her off to the mercenary Ganya Ivolgin, secretary to General Yepanchin (who has hopes of keeping her himself). Meanwhile, Rogozhin, too, has conceived a violent passion for Nastasya.

When Myshkin finally meets her, later that day, Nastasya takes him for a footman and scolds him for his incompetence. A party is held that night at her apartments at which Ferdyshchenko, the Ivolgins' boarder, proposes that everyone describe the worst thing he has ever done. In the middle of the game, Nastasya abruptly asks Myshkin whether she should go through with the marriage to Ganya, declaring that she will do whatever he bids her. The prince tells her not to marry, and she breaks off with Ganya and also releases Totsky. The party is then interrupted by the arrival of Rogozhin, who has brought the hundred thousand roubles he had promised Nastasya for her favors.

The plot of *The Idiot* is to revolve around Nastasya's desire to avenge her ruin *on herself*. She was taken advantage of by Totsky, but though her followers are legion, only the prince truly believes in her innocence. And though she would like to believe his account of her—"You've suffered and emerged pure out of such a hell, and that is a great deal"—she struggles with the fear that she will ruin him. Her self-lacerating outrage escalates at the party as she seems, hysterically, to accept Myshkin, then abruptly declares her intention of going with Rogozhin—even after the prince is discovered to have just come into a legacy of his own. Nastasya then takes Rogozhin's money and throws it into the fire, taunting Ganya to reach his hand in and save it. Ganya, pushed beyond endurance, faints.

Part II opens after a six-month gap in the narration during which, we later learn, Nastasya has repeatedly fled from Rogozhin to Myshkin, and back to Rogozhin. "Why, you don't think I'll murder her, do you?" Rogozhin asks the prince. In the same conversation, Myshkin absent-mindedly fingers the garden knife Rogozhin has been using to cut pages. Rogozhin then shows him his copy of Holbein's *Christ Taken from the Cross*. Rogozhin likes the painting, but Myshkin exclaims: "Why, some people may lose their faith by looking at that picture!"

Rogozhin suggests that he and Myshkin exchange crosses—in token of becoming brothers. He veers erratically between overtures to friendship and hostility, telling Myshkin before he leaves, "Take her, if that's how it is to be! She's yours!" But the prince is haunted by the feeling that he is being followed. On the stairs to his hotel, there is the flash of a knife and Rogozhin does indeed attack the prince—who is saved only by an epileptic spasm.

Myshkin's epilepsy is central to the book; indeed, as Elizabeth Dalton has observed, the plot itself is epileptic: "the action seems to progress unevenly, in waves of tension that gather and burst in climactic scenes of spectacular emotional violence, leaving the narrative energy of the novel depleted and for a time directionless, until a new wave of tension begins to accumulate."

Recovering in the country, Myshkin is confronted by friends of Burdovsky, who have concocted a plot to cheat the prince of his inheritance. The prince well understands that Burdovsky has been tricked, and wishes to settle a sum of money on him nonetheless. Hippolit, a dying young consumptive who is a member of the party, passionately condemns Myshkin: "more than anyone and more than anything in the world." Mrs. Yepanchin then confronts the prince about a letter he had written to Aglaya, which he replies was written "as to a sister."

As **Part III** opens, the possiblity that Myshkin and Aglaya may wed still hangs in the air. She is attracted to but also repelled by his simplicity, and suddenly bursts out: "I shall never, never marry him!" The prince protests that he never asked, and the incident is laughingly dismissed. Meanwhile Nastasya has been scheming to eliminate Aglaya's other suitor Radomsky, thereby leaving Aglaya free to marry Myshkin. When an army officer publicly insults Nastasya, however, the prince intercedes.

That night, at Myshkin's birthday party, Hippolit reads his "Necessary Explanation," a declaration of his intent to commit suicide. When he actually tries to shoot himself, however, at sunrise, the gun does not fire.

Aglaya now shows the prince Nastasya's letters begging her to marry him. Aglaya, unable to bear the rarefied quality of Myshkin's "love," urges him to go away with Nastasya.

At the beginning of **Part IV**, we learn that his sister Varya has been trying to arrange a match between Aglaya and Ganya. Myshkin finally asks for Aglaya's hand, and the Yepanchins throw an elaborate party to "test" him socially. There, however, Myshkin unleashes a tirade about Catholicism, becoming so excited that he has another seizure, knocking over a large Chinese vase.

On the next day Aglaya and Myshkin go to Nastasya, who demands that he choose between them. When Nastasya faints and the prince stays to tend to her without hesitation, the horrified Aglaya runs away.

The prince and Nastasya are now set to marry, but on her way to the church Nastasya spots Rogozhin in the crowd and abruptly runs away with him. Myshkin seeks out Rogozhin and is finally brought by him to the dead Nastasya, whom he has stabbed upon realizing she can never fully be his. The two men lie down side by side to keep an eerie vigil over the corpse; Myshkin's hubris—"a kind of hubris of submission," as one critic has called it—is thus implicated along with Rogozhin's passion in Nastasya's death. When they are found the next morning, the prince has relapsed into idiocy.

The Idiot is the most problematic of Dostoevsky's novels: Even after eight revisions the author himself, though deeply attached to it, could not escape a feeling of dissatisfaction with the result. One of its heroines is killed, another converts to Catholicism (a fate which the fanatically anti-Catholic Dostoevsky may well have considered worse than death); Rogozhin is sent to Siberia; and Myshkin, relapsed into idiocy, goes back to Switzerland. Romano Guardini has observed that "The whole book has the sound of death," and indeed, of the four major novels, *The Idiot* is the only one to end on a note of despair. ❁

List of Characters in
The Idiot

Myshkin is the kind and honest Russian prince who returns to St. Petersburg after undergoing treatment for a mental illness, and hopes to renew contact with his people. Naïve and childlike, he does not fit into the hypocritical Russian society. He falls in love with both Nastasya and Aglaya and must choose between them.

Rogozhin is the wealthy young man who travels back to St. Petersburg with Myshkin. Rash and impulsive, he is the complete opposite of Myshkin in nature and behavior. He falls madly in love with Nastasya and buys her for 100,000 rubles. He becomes Myshkin's foe after he finds out about Nastasya's love for Myshkin.

Nastasya Filippovna, though extremely beautiful, is vain and arrogant. She is brought up by Totsky who has an affair with her but later rejects her. She falls in love with Myshkin but runs away with Rogozhin because she does not want to ruin the Prince's life. She is murdered by Rogozhin when he realizes that she can never fully be his because of her love for Myshkin.

Aglaya is the youngest and prettiest daughter of General Yepanchin and Lizaveta Prokofyevna. Intelligent but emotional, she falls in love with Prince Myshkin but fails to express her love for him.

General Yepanchin is a shrewd man of the world who has accumulated his wealth through enterprise. He is proud of his family but tries to flirt with Nastasya.

Afnasy Ivanovitch Totsky is a wealthy landowner who seduces Nastasya and makes her his lover. Later, he becomes tired of her and offers to sell her to Ganya for a large sum of money.

Lizaveta Prokofyevna is the wife of General Yepanchin and mother of Alexandra, Adelaida, and Aglaya. Kind and generous, she befriends Prince Myshkin and remains his friend until the end.

Alexandra is the eldest daughter of General Yepanchin. Although charming and talented, she does not receive a marriage proposal like her sisters.

Adelaida is the second daughter of General Yepanchin who receives a marriage proposal from Prince S.

General Ivolgin is a drunkard who talks about imaginary episodes of his life. He is an embarrassment and a burden to his family.

Nina Alexandrovna, sensitive and dignified, is the wife of General Ivolgin and the mother of Ganya, Kolya, and Varya.

Ganya is the eldest son of General Ivolgin. He appears to be good but acts greedy as he agrees to marry Nastasya because of the wealth she would bring to the marriage.

Kolya is the youngest child of General Ivolgin who is friendly and helpful. He is on good terms with all the major characters and remains his father's main companion.

Varya is the sister of Ganya and Kolya who marries Ptitsyn to better her position in society. She befriends the Yepanchin girls in hopes of matching Aglaya and Ganya.

Ptitsyn is a sensible businessman who is a friend of Ganya. He marries Varya and allows the Ivolgin family to move into his house.

Madam Terentyev is General Ivolgin's mistress and Hippolit's mother.

Hippolit Terentyev, an eighteen-year-old consumptive, is the son of Madam Terentyev and friend of Kolya. He keeps talking about his impending death but lives through the end of the novel.

Ferdyshchenko is the friendly and gregarious boarder of the Ivolgins.

Lukyan Timmofeyitch Lebedev is the retired civil servant and widower who rents out his house to Prince Myshkin. He irritates everyone with his eccentric ways.

Vera Lebedev, kind and helpful, is the innocent and charming daughter of Lebedyev.

Keller is the boxer friend of Rogozin who writes a satirical pamphlet on the Prince but later tries to protect him. He admires Aglaya and desires to marry her.

Prince S is the wealthy and influential young man who marries Adelaida. ❀

Critical Views on
The Idiot

F. F. SEELEY ON NASTASYA

[F. F. Seeley has taught in the Department of Slavonic Studies at the University of Nottingham. His books include *Turgenev: A Reading of His Fiction* (1991), *From the Heyday of the Superfluous Man to Chekhov: Essays on 19th-Century Russian Literature* (1994), and *Saviour or Superman?: Old and New Essays on Tolstoy and Dostoevsky* (1999). Here, he shows how Nastasya Filippovna is more typical of a Dostoevsky hero than of a Dostoevsky heroine: enslaved by an idea, constantly testing her power (as when she throws the money in the fire), and ultimately destroying herself—"for her surrender to Rogozhin is equivalent to suicide, and suicide is for Dostoyevsky a crime."]

The hero is devoured, possessed by his 'idea'; so is Nastas'ya. The 'idea' by which she is driven to destruction is the 'idea' (or ideal) of purity. In violating this ideal Totsky had dealt her personality a deadly wound. The desecration of her ideal involved the shattering of her image of herself; even more, it involved the splitting of herself. It was not only that she had been 'pure' and had become, technically, 'impure'; it was not only the affront to her dignity as a human being: however deep that wound, it must have been scarred over, if not by time, then by her no less deep contempt for her seducer; nor was it only her social disgrace; nor even the combination of all these factors. It was more serious than that: Totsky (as is made explicit in just two words[24] which escape her at her name-day party, and of course appears implicit in half of all that happens thereafter) had unleashed in her passions of which she had been unaware, which she hated and was ashamed of: had, in fact, created in her the nucleus of a potential second personality, since her cult of purity would not allow her to accept and absorb these new passions into her original self. Here is the essence of the 'idea' of Dostoyevsky's heroes too: the 'idea' is a conceptual formulation of a complex of desires or passions which are unacceptable to the dominant self and so are repressed and banished to the unconscious. ⟨. . .⟩

⟨. . .⟩ Myshkin enters, and with him Rogozhin re-enters, her life—to confront her with the pressing need to choose between her two personalities. ⟨. . .⟩

Nastas'ya's attitude ⟨to both⟩ is riddled with ambivalences. The wild recklessness of Rogozhin's passion called out to the part of her which she herself had designated 'the woman of the streets', 'Rogozhin's woman'. At the same time it repelled and revolted her pristine self. Moreover, she was impelled towards him by the compulsive urge to punish or destroy herself, against which her instinct to cling to life and happiness struggled with fluctuating success.

Even more complex was the conflict of her emotions in relation to Myshkin; marriage to him was a prospect which both tempted and terrified. She was drawn to him by his belief in her, by his respect and devotion; she was desperately eager to see herself as he saw her and to accept herself as he accepted her; but her ideal, her obsession with purity made this impossible save for brief periods at long intervals. Then, when she realised his love for Aglaya, she set herself to bring them together; but the strident clumsiness of the means which she adopted revealed, behind her sincere desire to secure his happiness by her own self-sacrifice, an unconscious urge to triumph both over the virtuous young lady by making her a present of 'her man', and over Myshkin himself by bestowing on him the happiness which he had failed to give herself. She also saw Myshkin as a child, and to that her reactions were equally contradictory. On the one hand, it appealed to her thirst for purity and to her disgust with the sort of relations between men and women which had prevailed in her experience up till then. On the other hand, she was horrified by the prospect of 'ruining' him. What did she mean by 'ruining'? If her fear was of ruining him socially, it seems absurdly exaggerated. Two other factors seem to be involved. First, a metaphysical dread of contaminating his childlike purity with her impurity; this would be conscious. Second, a probably unconscious doubt as to whether he was not too much of a child to be able to satisfy the other half of her nature—the half which Totsky had awakened. In this connexion, it is worth recalling Rogozhin's words to Myshkin: 'Even as I now love her, so she now loves another. And that other . . . is you!' If Nastas'ya had come to love Myshkin with the wild passion of a Rogozhin, how could she have hoped for a response in kind? And so, unable to choose either between her two selves or between the two men who loved her, she fled desperately from one to the other and back again, till she found in death a refuge from all need to decide or choose.

Note
²⁴ . . . *raspalit, razvratit* . . . (Part I, ch. xvi).

—F. F. Seeley, "Dostoyevsky's Women," *The Slavonic and East European Review* XXXIX, no. 93 (1961): pp. 305–8.

ROGER L. COX ON EXECUTION, EPILEPSY, AND APOCALYPSE

[Roger L. Cox is Professor Emeritus of English at the University of Delaware, and author of *Between Earth and Heaven: Shakespeare, Dostoevsky, and the Meaning of Christian Tragedy* (1969) and *Shakespeare's Comic Changes: The Time-Lapse Metaphor as Plot Device* (1991). In this extract, Cox considers the novel's use of the imagery of falling and light (both of which permeate the Book of Revelation)—and final as well as recurring experiences of the end of the world (execution and epilepsy, respectively)—to together convey Myshkin's vision of Christian apocalypse, when "There will be no more time."]

⟨. . .⟩ When a man puts on "the whole armor of God," including the "helmet of salvation" and the "shield of faith," how can the artist portray him as an individual? How does he reveal the man *inside* the suit of armor? ⟨. . .⟩

Dostoevsky's method for rendering intelligible the vision that is graven on Myshkin's heart is to bring together several kinds of experience which, though they may be unfamiliar to the reader, can at least be made understandable in realistic terms. The first of these involves the agony, the intense emotions and perceptions, of a person as he suffers through the last moments before his execution; and the instrument for execution in *The Idiot* is not the firing squad or even the gallows, but the guillotine. ⟨. . .⟩

⟨. . .⟩ The moment of vision and urgency when one lives in the awareness that his death is both imminent and certain cannot be prolonged. "For some reason it is impossible," but that moment can be represented as *recurring* and thereby renewing its effect in a man's life. Hence, the second kind of experience that is associated with Myshkin is an effort to communicate the vision which is "graven on his heart"—his epilepsy. ⟨. . .⟩

⟨. . .⟩ Obviously, Dostoevsky insists in both cases upon the significance of the moment, the paramount importance of time as it slips away. But far more effective is the highly dramatic scene in which Rogozhin assaults Myshkin with a knife, fully intending to kill him, and in so doing precipitates an epileptic fit. Here the emotions of the man about to be killed and the feelings of the epileptic are literally identified with each other. ⟨. . .⟩

The two kinds of experience are fused ⟨. . .⟩ not only by coincidence in time, but by imagery as well. The "intense *inner* light," the "gleams and flashes of the highest sensation of life and self-consciousness" which are associated with the epileptic fit recall the earlier description of the man led out to execution and then reprieved, who looks around during what he thinks are his last moments: "Not far off there was a church, and the gilt roof was glittering in the bright sunshine. He remembered that he stared very persistently at that roof and the light flashing from it; he could not tear himself away from the light. It seemed to him that those rays were his new nature and that in three minutes be would somehow melt into them." The epileptic scream brings to mind the footman's question, when Myshkin first describes the execution of a French criminal, "Do they scream?" ⟨. . .⟩

⟨. . .⟩ Myshkin apprehends such a moment as both final and recurring; what he feels is as compelling as anything imposed from the outside, yet it is wholly internal. ⟨. . .⟩

More important than the apocalyptic imagery is the apocalyptic eschatology. Any discussion of eschatology necessarily involves a consideration of time, with its divisions into past, present, and future. ⟨. . .⟩ The Apocalypse gets over this difficulty by referring to God (twice in the first chapter) as the one "who is and who was and who is to come." ⟨. . .⟩ ⟨T⟩he point is not simply that "time is precious," as Madame Epanchin moralizes when Myshkin is trying to explain himself. The point is rather that in the moment of vision one apprehends past, present, and future as a single entity—Christ's sufferings are not past but present, and the judgment upon man is not off in the future somewhere; it is *now*.

But paradoxically, if a man participates in the sufferings of Christ, in the apocalyptic moment he is not only judged, but forgiven. 〈...〉 Most characters in *The Idiot* are ready to judge, and a few are ready to forgive, but only Myshkin (despite Aglaia's claim) stands ready, by virtue of the vision graven upon his heart, to judge and to forgive, to be judged and to be forgiven. 〈...〉

—Roger L. Cox, *Between Earth and Heaven: Shakespeare, Dostoevsky, and the Meaning of Christian Tragedy* (New York: Holt, Rinehart and Winston, 1969): pp. 166, 169, 170–71, 172, 178, 179–80.

Michael Holquist on Teleology

[Michael Holquist (b. 1935) is Professor of Slavic Languages and Literatures and Chairman of the Department of Comparative Literature at Yale University. He is the author of *Dialogism: Bakhtin and His World* (1990) and editor of several volumes of Bakhtin's essays. Here, he examines the Christian view of time, and its role in a novel where the "horror consists [not in apocalypse] but rather in the discovery that there *are* no ends that give meaning, just as there are no beginnings."]

A basic peculiarity of the Christian attitude toward time 〈...〉 is that in it, "the center of interest is neither at the beginning, as it was for the Greeks, nor at the end as it is in evolutionary theories, but in the middle." Christ is conceived as an eruption of eternal order into the temporal sequence. The momentary simultaneity of these two strata of time, which Christ made possible, resulted in a cutoff between the "horizontal" segments of time we designate B.C. and A.D. 〈...〉

The difficulty of finding a common term that will serve to connect otherwise discrete moments—conceived as an existential rather than historiographical dilemma—we have seen dramatized in the central metaphor of Myshkin's epilepsy: his inability to join health and illness, the moment of ecstacy that precedes his fits with the awful minutes he spends writhing on the ground in the grip of the epileptic attack itself. ⟨...⟩

⟨...⟩ The split between the "before" and "after" that Nastasya Filipovna cannot connect is marked by her seduction. ⟨...⟩

⟨...⟩ She never succeeds in recapturing *otradnoe*, and so the two parts of her life are as marked off from each other as the opened versus the as-yet-uncut pages of the copy of Solovyov she gives Rogozhin. The reason for so radical a split in her biography is that she attaches transcendent significance to her existence before the seduction: like the open pages of the book, it was full of meaning. On the other hand, the years after the seduction are as meaningless as the closed pages of that book. The inability to overcome this gap drives her on to ever more hysterical attempts to wipe out the *otradnoe* origin with a new beginning, until, in despair, she gives herself to Rogozhin's knife—a Garden-of-Eden knife that separates the open and closed pages of a history book. ⟨...⟩

⟨...⟩ The three major figures of the novel—Myshkin, Rogozhin, and Nastasya Filipovna—are all fatherless. The other characters must all in their own way confront the failure of the fathers. ⟨...⟩

The collapse of bridges between generations is marked in *The Idiot* by the failure of material inheritance. It will be remembered that money, which plays so enormous a role in the novel, always comes from the wills of a dead generation. ⟨...⟩

The major symbol clusters of the novel—execution, the Holbein Christ, epilepsy, Don Quixote, money—swirl around a core that is common to them all: the failure of *kairos* to effect *chronos*. There is no wholeness that will remain unsplintered throughout its unfolding in time: the man who promises to change his life if not executed in the next second, continues—when spared—to lead the same existence as before, the meaninglessness of which was clear from the vantage point of that exalted moment before the firing squad (i, ii). The promise of Christ's life is denied in the painting of his death: the cycle of biological time is unbroken: the Prince's moment of lucid self-awareness is wiped out in the epileptic fit that follows it. All the money, all the inheritances lead to a cutoff between past and present. No essence can withstand the battering of the moments as they pass by. The structure of a single moment's promise broken under the onslaught of a series of other such moments following upon it, constitutes the novel's central pattern. Its most paradigmatic expression is in the failure of *Heilsgeschichte:* Christ did not change the course of history; his promise of peace has been eroded by all the wars ever since. It is the collapse of this messianic legacy in the past that underlies all the other failed testaments from father to son in the book. Without the Christian inheritance, at a time when the *imitatio Christi* breaks down, each man must find his own way, seek his own identity without the aid of preexisting models. He must, in other words, become an idiot in the root sense of that word—someone on his own.

—Michael Holquist, *Dostoevsky and the Novel* (Princeton: Princeton University Press, 1977): pp. 107, 114, 118, 119, 122–23.

Elizabeth Dalton on Dostoevsky and the Unconscious

[In this extract from *Unconscious Structure in* The Idiot: *A Study in Literature and Psychoanalysis,* Elizabeth Dalton provides a reading of Myshkin and Rogozhin as a unique pair of Dostoevskian "doubles," one all superego, the other all id. She then shows that the narrative is itself controlled by a kind of epilepsy: "It is into the darkness that lies beyond the controls of the ego, the perilous region of unmodified instinct and savage retaliation, that we are invited by the great scenes of mounting tension and final frenzy and collapse."]

⟨. . .⟩ Myshkin and Rogozhin stand along with Stavrogin and Verkhovensky, Raskolnikov and Svidrigailov, and the two Golyadkins in the long series of Dostoevsky's doubles. ⟨. . .⟩

⟨. . .⟩ The contrast between them evokes a more primitive mode of thought and appeals to a deeper and more archaic layer of the mind than that suggested by the other pairs. Myshkin and Rogozhin are related as a thing may be represented by its contrary in a dream, as primal words have antithetical meanings, as the masochist is also a sadist. Their relationship suggests that even tendencies that are perceived in consciousness as entirely opposed—such as lust and purity, or aggression and passivity—may be only different aspects of a single entity in the unconscious. ⟨...⟩

⟨T⟩he brilliant, unlimited, harmonious vision that comes to Myshkin during the pre-epileptic aura is a regression to the timeless world of the primitive ego, buried in the oldest layers of the mind and illuminated during the instant of the aura like a dark landscape in a flash of lightning. ⟨...⟩

The moment of the aura is virtually the only point in *The Idiot* at which instinctual impulses break through the barriers of repression with sufficient force to be felt in direct, unmodified form as pleasurable and gratifying. At this point the sexual and aggressive feelings usually experienced by Myshkin in the disguised masochistic form of suffering rush into the ego with an effect of ecstatic and joyful release. But the ego cannot tolerate the force of these energies in their original unmodified form, nor can it allow their meaning to rise into conscious awareness. The moment of orgiastic release is followed by the total eclipse of the ego in the epileptic seizure. The fit is also the revenge of the superego, which can be deposed only temporarily; for the uninhibited release of sexual and aggressive energy it exacts the talion penalty of symbolic castration and death. The instinctual drives are once more experienced under the negative sign of superego, in the form of asceticism and suffering. ⟨...⟩

⟨The⟩ moments of heightened consciousness represent a breakthrough beyond the barriers of repression that define the normal conditions of the ego into a state in which the darker regions of personality usually inaccessible to consciousness are illuminated and the sense of existence is immeasurably intensified. The ego experiences these states as an enormous expansion of its capacity: the conscious mind appears to be offered the possibility of penetrating a limitless reality. In these scenes the reader feels as if he is being forced to *know* more and more, as if the mind is being wrenched out of its limits and into those areas of experience of which no rational understanding is possible. The aim of these passages seems to be to push consciousness to and beyond the breaking point, as if to attain something like the state of that head severed on the guillotine: freed from the limitations of its normal state, perhaps that isolated head achieves some last awful moment of total comprehension, some final transcendence of the barrier between the conscious and the unconscious mind, even between life and death.

The condition of this final knowledge is, of course, annihilation. ⟨...⟩

> —Elizabeth Dalton, *Unconscious Structure in* The Idiot: *A Study in Literature and Psychoanalysis* (Princeton: Princeton University Press, 1979): pp. 83, 86, 133, 138–39.

Plot Summary of
Demons (The Possessed)

Its cast of terrorists, the Dostoevskian "polyphony" of its voices, and the endless night of the plot combine to make *Demons* the most unnerving of the major novels. Unlike *Crime and Punishment,* as John Jones notes, it lacks "the astral, feathering humour of America, anatomy, and ordinary ghosts"; and its most striking character—Nikolai Stavrogin, the "center that disappears—achieves what seems a perfect nihilism." (Commenting on the terrible purity of Stavrogin's detachment, F. F. Seeley was to note drily that pedophilia is not a taste.)

Demons was inspired by the 1869 murder of a student by the "Nechaev group" of dissidents. The novel both begins and ends with Stepan Trofimovitch, a liberal idealist of the 1840s (and, it would seem, harmless poseur) who is hired by his longtime patroness, Varvara Stavrogin, as tutor for her son Nikolai Stavrogin. Stepan's pedagogical methods are distinctly peculiar, and his comic relationship with Varvara is replete with a melodrama of which neither seems aware.

When Stavrogin finally returns from his regiment, at 25, he has already fought several duels, redeeming himself with subsequent promotions. He is beautiful to the point of repulsiveness, his face "like a mask"; the local ladies are "sharply divided into two parties—one party adored him, the other hated him to the point of blood vengeance; but both lost their minds."

Stavrogin pulls two bizarre stunts, grabbing one man's nose and biting another's ear. In Paris he had befriended Liza, the daughter of his mother's friend; but Varvara, wary of an attraction between Nikolai and her ward Dasha (the sister of Shatov, Dostoevsky's philosophical surrogate), hurriedly arranges to marry Dasha off to Stepan.

Approached by Marya Timofeyevna, the lame sister of Lebyadkin (who had been courting Liza), Varvara takes her home. At the house they find Stepan and Shatov with the narrator ("G——v"), and are joined by Liza's mother and Dasha and later by Lebyadkin. When Stepan's son Peter and Stavrogin arrive, Varvara asks Stavrogin if

Marya is his wife, and he denies it—though it is perfectly true. Marya had become infatuated with Stavrogin, explains Peter, and he "whimsically" married her but never consummated the marriage. Peter also unwittingly reveals that Stepan had spoken of his engagement to Dasha as "marrying someone else's sins"; Varvara, furious, banishes him. Shatov suddenly hits Stavrogin in the face. When he has gone, Liza faints.

In **Part II** we find that Peter has gained an ascendancy over the wife of the governor, von Lembke, and is spearheading a political faction to be bound in blood by the killing of one of its members.

We now learn more about the ideas of Kirillov, who lives with Shatov. Kirillov insists that "Everything is good, everything," but has formed the fantastic idea of becoming God through the act of suicide. Stavrogin also meets with Shatov, who urges him to find God by returning to the soil but who, when questioned about his faith, is himself able to muster only an "I . . . I will believe in God." Though a reactionary, he is as ineluctably drawn to Stavrogin as Peter: "I cannot tear you out of my heart, Nikolai Stavrogin!" Stavrogin "warns" him there may be a plot against his life by the circle (consisting, in actuality, only of Peter), and Shatov sends him to the retired bishop, Tikhon. The account of their meeting—and of Stavrogin's confession to the rape of a fourteen-year-old, who then killed herself—was excised by censors and is generally printed as an appendix to the novel. As many critics have noted, it in fact weakens the character, and the novel, to hear Stavrogin "confess," and so the chapter is best read as separate from the novel proper.

On his way to see Lebyadkin, Stavrogin comes upon Fedka the Convict, a former serf, and they quarrel. Lebyadkin threatens to turn traitor and expose the circle. On his way home, Stavrogin encounters Fedka again and throws money at him which Fedka accepts, taking it as payment to kill Lebyadkin.

Stavrogin now fights a duel with the son of Gaganov, whose nose he had pulled, firing in the air. Dasha, whom he sees afterward, reaffirms her devotion.

Peter, meanwhile, convenes the meeting of the revolutionaries at Virginsky's house. They all—except Stavrogin—believe Peter to be an agent from Europe, assigned to coordinate these revolutionaries' cells. Peter proposes that every man present answer a question: if he knew of a conspiracy to a political murder, would he turn informer? Shatov leaves; Stavrogin declines to respond; and someone points out that even Peter himself had only asked the question, but did not answer it. Peter afterward tells Stavrogin he is to be made their "Ivan the Tsarevich," leader of this first cell which, Peter believes, will be only the inauguration of many more. Peter also hints at killing Marya, and will subsequently implicate his father as a ringleader of the circle.

As **Part III** begins, there have been outbreaks of arson and violence all over the province. The literary gala organized by von Lembke's wife, under the tutelage of Peter, is finally held, culminating in a speech by Karmazinov, a not-so-veiled version of Dostoevsky's anti-Slavophil rival Turgenev. Fedka has set fires along the river; Marya and Lebyadkin are found dead.

Urged by Stavrogin to elope, Liza tells him: "It has always seemed to me that you would bring me to some place where there lives a huge, evil spider, as big as a man, and we would spend our whole life there looking at him and being afraid. That's how our mutual love would pass . . ." Peter arrives and announces the murders of Marya and her brother, and Stavrogin admits to Liza that while he didn't kill them, he failed to prevent their killings. Liza and her fiancé, Mavriky, set out for the Lebyadkins,' where she is set upon by a mob as "Stavrogin's woman," and killed.

At a second meeting, Peter urges the murder of Shatov to protect the cell; Kirillov, he explains, has agreed to take the blame. The revolutionaries feel, in Peter's control, "like they [have] suddenly been caught like flies in the web of a huge spider"—a phrase recalling Liza's words to Stavrogin—but they agree. Fedka is also to die.

Shatov's former wife arrives and gives birth to a child by Stavrogin. Shatov tends to both and, after leaving to meet the group, is murdered by Peter—who now also admits that they are not part of a terrorist network, but are in fact a lone cell. Stepan, meanwhile, undergoes a deathbed conversion.

Shatov's wife realizes he has been killed, and dies soon after. The circle is now in a shambles and its members, including Peter, are arrested. Stavrogin summons Darya; when she and Varvara find him, however, he has hanged himself.

Though Kirillov had duly committed suicide, most of the disillusioned revolutionaries cooperate with police, one even falling to the floor "squealing"—an echo of the passage about the Gerasene demoniac, from Luke, which Stepan had asked to hear before he died, and which had opened the novel as one of two epigraphs. *Demons,* for all its seemingly unrelieved bleakness, ends ultimately on a note of hope: for as Richard Pevear has noted, "the Nechaevs of the novel, Petrusha Verkhovensky and the rest, turn out in both comparisons to be, not demons, not demoniacs, but the herd of swine." With their destruction, indeed, only with their destruction, the "sick man"—Russia—can be healed. ❀

List of Characters in
Demons (The Possessed)

Stepan Trofimovitch (Verkhovensky) is a widower who has been married twice and is the father of Pyotr Stepanovich, who was given to his aunts to be raised. He tutors younger students and lectures at local universities, but is constantly plagued by financial problems. His inability to maintain financial stability causes him to become dependent on Varvara.

Varvara Petrovna is a wealthy widow with one son, Nikolai. She is recognized as a woman with high social standing and is active in local politics. She begins to assist Stepan financially and controls many aspects of his life, including his wardrobe. Stepan appreciates her sponsorship and the exposure he receives to the social life of the town.

Nikolai Stavrogin is a former student of Stepan who returns home to reside with his mother, Varvara after traveling abroad. He does not take advantage of the opportunities his mother provides for him and his obnoxious behavior discredits him in society. Nikolai's wild behavior causes him to be diagnosed with insanity and his mother sends him away to restore her socialite reputation. He secretly marries Marya and has affairs with numerous women.

Peter Verhovensky (Stepanovich) is the son of Stepan and establishes a political group. He is an effective speaker who always says what people want to hear and is never at a loss for words. His arrogant and deceitful ways are apparent but overlooked by the community. He is able to quickly establish himself as a regular on the social scene, winning the devotion of the governor's wife by playing the fool.

Shatov is a former student who was expelled from school due to an unknown scandal. He was tutored by Stepan in childhood and was greatly indebted to Varvara. Once a radical socialist, he becomes a Russian idealist. He tries to break out of the group but fails and is killed.

Kirillov is an atheist who supports the revolutionary movement. He is sincere and willing to sacrifice his life for the group whenever they call upon him.

Liputin is a known liberal and has the reputation of being an atheist. He thrives on gossip in Stephan's meetings and is also heavily involved in Pyotr's organization.

Virginsky is a self-taught well educated man. He is a staunch liberal and a member of the group, although according to Stepan he jumped on the liberal bandwagon.

Lebyadkin is new to the town but wins the heart of Virginsky's wife and quickly moves into their house. He is a drunkard who beats his sister and has a poor reputation in the community.

Fedka was once a serf belonging to Pyotr. He is willing to murder for money and the group uses his services.

Darya (Dasha) is Shatov's sister and Varvara's ward. She possesses a gentle nature and is very altruistic.

Liza Tushina, beautiful and wealthy, is the daughter of the Drozdovs and a relative of the governor's wife. She was the student of Stepan as a young girl and has had a relationship with Stavrogin, which she was never able to get over.

Marya Timofeyevna is a cripple who is married to Stavrogin and is the sister of Lebyadkin. She is abused and mentally unstable. ❁

Critical Views on
Demons (The Possessed)

Philip Rahv on Russia's Demons

[Philip Rahv (1908–1973) was an influential critic and a founding editor of *Partisan Review*. His books include *Image and Idea: Fourteen Essays on Literary Themes* (1949), *Literature and the Sixth Sense* (1969), and *Essays on Literature and Politics, 1932–1972* (1978). Here, he considers the significance of *Demons* in Russian political history.]

The fact is that it really contains two novels. It was begun as a "tendencious" study of the evolution of ideas from fathers to sons, of the development of the liberal idealism of the thirties and forties of the last century into the nihilism and socialism of the sixties and seventies; but Dostoevsky encountered such difficulties in its writing that he finally fused it with his projected *Life of a Great Sinner*, which was to be his major effort on the subject of atheism. For that reason *The Possessed* has two distinct sets of characters, one sacred and one profane, one metaphysical and one empirical—the group around Stavrogin, the great sinner, and the group around the Verhovenskys, father and son, who are defined politically. While one set commits sins, the other commits crimes. Externally—in his melodramatic, sinister attractiveness and in the Byronic stress given to his personal relations—Stavrogin derives from early European Romanticism, but in his moral sensuality, in his craving for remorse and martyrdom, he is an authentic member of the Karamazov family. He is doubled within himself as well as through Shatov and Kirillov, his satellites in the story. Shatov represents his Russian, national-messianic side, and Kirillov his experiments with God. ⟨...⟩

In *The Possessed* liberalism receives the broadest and most perspicacious criticism in the history of the novel. The malevolence with which the portrait of the intellectual Stepan Trofimovitch, the elder Verhovensky, is executed, in no way detracts from its enduring reality and social truth. ⟨...⟩

A gentleman pacifist and esthete, he simultaneously shines the boots of reaction and revolution. His standing protest he makes by lying down; he is subtle in his feelings, a self-indulgent humanitarian, and a parasite. His author created him with unsurpassed verve, wholly persuading us that his creation is objective. He is superior to Thomas Mann's Settembrini, whose distant relative he is, for he is understood not argumentatively but through a tangible social milieu. Dostoevsky boldly reduces him to his primary political elements while holding him together on the spiritual plane in a delicate equilibrium. And what a hazardous yet just simplification it was to place him in the position of being the charge of a rich and patrician lady, of making an assertive dramatic image out of her financial support of him. This exchange of cash and culture, however, is not conceived as a simple transaction; on the contrary, it entails mutual distrust, bitterness, and emotional tempests—but in the end a sentimental reconciliation is effected. In virtually the same terms Trotsky defines the basic relation of the intellectuals to the bourgeoisie in his *Literature and Revolution*. ⟨...⟩

The biographers of Dostoevsky tell us that the activity of Pyotr Verhovensky's circle in *The Possessed* is an imaginative imitation of the Nechayev episode in Russian revolutionary history. Now in Nechayevism the Russian revolution had its first taste of Machiavellian deception and double-dealing. Just as Verhovensky acted without principle and out of relation to any definite theory of social reconstruction, so Nechayev believed that it was his "exclusive task to destroy the existing system—to build up is not our task." ⟨...⟩

⟨...⟩ Since he has no real historic validity, Nechayev-Verhovensky is stripped of moral norms. ⟨...⟩

⟨His⟩ attempt to overthrow the Czar without the active intervention of the masses is equivalent to Stalin's attempt to build socialism in Russia in isolation from the fate of the international working class. The Marxist movement, on the other hand, distinguishes itself from the Jacobin and Blanquist types in that it is "the first one in the history of class societies which in all its factors is calculated upon the organization and initiative of the masses" (Luxemburg). The strong resemblance between Nechayev-Verhovensky and Stalin-Yezhov is to be explained, to my mind, by the coincident manifestations of two specific phases in Russian politics. *If Nechayevism represents the pre-Marxist stage of the revolution, Stalinism represents its post-Marxist one.*

—Philip Rahv, "Dostoevsky and Politics: Notes on 'The Possessed,'" *Partisan Review* V, no. 2 (1938): pp. 25–26, 29, 30, 31, 32.

Vyacheslav Ivanov on Marya

[Among the works by Vyacheslav Ivanov (1866–1949) available in English are *Freedom and the Tragic Life: A Study in Dostoevsky* (1952), *Correspondence Across a Room* (with Mikhail Osipovich Gershenzon, 1984), and *Selected Essays* (2001). In this extract, Ivanov examines the role of Marya Timofeyevna in the myth, with its strong echoes of Faust, that Dostoevsky sought to weave around the destiny of the Russian earth—that enchanted bride awaiting its final deliverance and transformation into "Holy Russia."]

In *The Possessed* Dostoevsky tried to show how the eternally-feminine principle in the Russian soul has to suffer violence and oppression at the hands of those Daemons who in the people contend against Christ for the mastery of the masculine principle in the people's consciousness.[1] He sought to show how these Daemons, in their attack upon the Russian soul, also wound the Mother of God herself (as shown in the symbolic episode of the desecration of the ikon), although their vilifications cannot reach her invisible depths (compare the symbol of the untouched silver garment of the Virgin Undefiled in the home of the murdered Maria Timofeyevna). Since the basic theme of the novel is the symbolism of the relationship between the Earth's soul, the dating, erring human spirit and the Powers of Evil, it was quite natural that Dostoevsky should be confronted by a presentation of this myth which had already been attempted in the world's literature—although with a different orientation, and without any allusion to the idea of the mission of the Redeemer: namely, in Goethe's *Faust*.[2]

Maria Timofeyevna took the place of Gretchen; who, after the disclosures in the second part of the tragedy, is identified, as a manifestation of the eternally-feminine, both with Helen and with Mother Earth. Nicolai Stavrogin is the Russian Faust: but in a negative version, since love has been quenched in him, and, with it, the indefatigable striving—erotic, in the Platonic sense—through which Faust is saved. ⟨...⟩

She who sings the song of love in her inward cell is not only a "medium" of Mother Earth (the late Hellenic scholars who classified ecstasies and trances would have called her "one possessed by Earth"⟨...⟩), but also Mother Earth's symbol. In the myth she represents the soul of earth, under the specific aspect of Russian earth. That is why she has her little mirror in her hand—the universal soul is perpetually reflected in Nature. Moreover, it is not accidental that she is the wedded wife of the protagonist of the tragedy, Nicolai Stavrogin. Nor is it accidental that she is not truly his wife, but retains her virginity. ⟨...⟩

Even Maria's lameness is a sign of her secret guilt of hostility to God[3]: the guilt of a half-heartedness and disloyalty that perhaps were present in her from the beginning; or, at least, of imperfect loyalty, of a primordial resistance to the bridegroom who deserted her, as Eros deserts Psyche—who, because of an original sin inherent in her mortal being, is sinful in the sight of the Divine love. ⟨...⟩

From an early age—probably ever since his years of imprisonment—Dostoevsky had pondered over the spiritual mission of the Russian people. Later he speaks of "the independent Russian idea", which his homeland must "bring forth with fearful pangs", and even refers to its "labour-pains" as having already begun.

The riddle propounded in that prophetically inspired work, *The Possessed*, is connected with the nexus of problems contained in this expectation. What is the spiritual meaning of the secret yearning of the Russian Earth for Redemption and the Redeemer? How will the coming of the hero in Christ, her Ivan the Tsarevich—heralded in her prophetic dreams of her God-bearing mission—how will this coming manifest itself? In other words, how can the land of "wise will and wild action", which for ages has been entitled "holy", become indeed "Holy Russia", and the people become the Church? How does a thing, impossible for man, become possible for God?

Notes

[1] "Whence come the Nihilists? They come from nowhere, for they have always been with us, in us, and around us."—*From Dostoevsky's Notes.*

[2] Goethe's influence on Dostoevsky can be detected even in the latter's early work, *The Insulted and Injured.* In creating Nelly, Dostoevsky may have had in

mind the image of Mignon.
³ Concerning lameness as the mystical sign of the fight with God, see *Genesis* xxxii, 24–32.
—Vyacheslav Ivanov, *Freedom and the Tragic Life: A Study in Dostoevsky,* Norman Cameron, trans. (London: Harvill Press, 1952): pp. 60–63, 69.

JOHN JONES ON "AT TIKHON'S"

[John Jones's (b. 1924) books include *The Egotistical Sublime: A History of Wordsworth's Imagination* (1954), *On Aristotle and Greek Tragedy* (1962), and *John Keats's Dream of Truth* (1969). Here, he suggests that the excluded chapter "At Tikhon's" be read as a footnote—and not to *Demons*, but to *Crime and Punishment*. Dostoevsky slips here into Raskolnikov, there into Svidrigailov, yet never succeeds in truly reaching Stavrogin; thus the eerie, haunting quality of the novel's "center that disappears."]

⟨I⟩n these pages, instead of brushing past Raskolnikov and Svidrigailov in his return upon the underground man, Dostoevsky has allowed himself to be obstructed by them, and the result is a Stavrogin who compounds Raskolnikov's bracing himself to enter the police station '*as a man*' and confess with Svidrigailov's reaching out in all directions, including the far extremes of moral and physical debauchery, in the hope that something, it doesn't matter what, will make him unbored.

After a sleepless night Stavrogin sets forth. Then outside the monastery where Bishop Tikhon lives, 'he stopped, hastily and anxiously felt something in his side pocket and smiled'.³⁸ That is Raskolnikov's smile. We know it well. And the gesture is Raskolnikov's too, for example when he feels for the axe slung inside his overcoat.³⁹ Even the sudden stopping is tell-tale. Stavrogin would never stop in the street like that, his psychophysical being is other. ⟨...⟩

⟨...⟩ Since 'At Tikhon's' is constantly referred to in Russia and the West as Stavrogin's Confession, it occurs to me to note that the word confession does not appear anywhere in the chapter. ⟨...⟩ Stavrogin's prodigal scattering of reasons does more than leave the question open. It leaves all questioning behind. ⟨...⟩

⟨...⟩ Everybody, including the present Soviet editor, talks about Stavrogin's forcing or rape of a young girl.⁴⁵ So to sort the thing out: Stavrogin has designs on the child; he kisses her hand, puts her on his knee, whispers to her. She is in terror. Then

> At last there occurred, suddenly, a most strange event which I shall never forget and which astonished me: the little girl flung her arms round my neck and in a rush began kissing me frenziedly. Her face expressed complete rapture. I nearly got up and went away out of pity, I found this so unpleasant in a slip of a child. But I overcame my immediate fearful feeling, and I stayed.⁴⁶

And that's that. The next sentence begins a new paragraph: 'When all was over, she was covered in confusion.' Therefore no rape occurs. The child is sexually responsive and perhaps dominant. Hence her smile 'as if ashamed, a kind of twisted smile' after her terror and immediately before the passage I have just quoted. Hence, later, her words 'I have killed God', and her suicide. Getting this right obviously matters in itself, but also for its bearing on two further issues.

First, it drives Stavrogin even closer to Svidrigailov than I have suggested so far. The episode with the child is a reworking of Svidrigailov's nightmare. ⟨...⟩

Second, it discredits those ⟨...⟩ who seek to explain Dostoevsky's failure to 'reinstate' 'At Tikhon's' solely by the prevailing conditions of censorship.⁴⁸ He got Svidrigailov's nightmare past the censor, and there is a good deal more to that horror than I have quoted; and 'At Tikhon's' could have been got past him too. ⟨...⟩

⟨...⟩ Tikhon and Stavrogin have both got it right. But this *it* cannot be said, can only be shown forth as in the suicide letter where Stavrogin writes 'My desires are too weak; they cannot guide me.' We aim straight at the art of *The Possessed* by observing that the follow-up, I'm a lukewarm man, or I'm an indifferent, an apathetic man, is beyond Stavrogin. All self-definition, as Dostoevsky finally shaped and gave Stavrogin to the world, is beyond him. That is why, instead of taking the weakness of his desires to himself, Stavrogin continues in figurative, musing vein, sad and free, very beautiful in context:

'You can cross a river on a tree-trunk, but not on a chip of wood.' This is the same young man who bit the ear of the governor—and we can only meet and get to know him in the novel itself.

Get to know as opposed to get at. The 'At Tikhon's' chapter, rejected by the editor and finally abandoned by the novelist, gets at, ponders the case of, somebody we never even meet there: the smiling man outside the monastery is Raskolnikov, and the document in his pocket recounts Svidrigailov's deeds.

Notes
[38] *PSS*, Vol. XI, p. 5.
[39] p. 67.
[45] *PSS*, Vol. XII, pp. 241, 244. He also writes of Stavrogin's 'confession' throughout. Neither confession nor sexual violence are mentioned in any of the manuscript variants of the 'At Tikhon's' chapter.
[46] Ibid., Vol. XI, p. 16.
[48] Ibid., Vol. XII, p. 237.

—John Jones, *Dostoevsky* (Oxford: Clarendon Press, 1983): pp. 260, 262–64, 265–66.

N. N. Shneidman on Suicide and Freedom

[N. N. Shneidman is Professor Emeritus of Slavic Languages and Literatures at the University of Toronto. He is the author of *Soviet Literature in the 1980's: Decade of Transition* (1989), *Russian Literature, 1988–1994: The End of an Era* (1995), and *Jerusalem of Lithuania: The Rise and Fall of Jewish Vilnius, a Personal Perspective* (1998). In this exact he delineates the proto-existential paradox enacted by Kirillov, who like Christ "sacrifices himself out of love for man. But his sacrifice has to show man his ultimate destiny and his terrible freedom from God. Thus Kirillov usurps the place of Christ and aspires to replace him in the universe, a fact which points, according to K. Mochulsky, to Kirillov's irrational need for God."]

⟨W⟩e are presented in the novel with a psychological autopsy of a would-be suicide who makes no secret of his intentions and who reveals to the outside world the motives which drive him to self-destruction. In addition, Kirillov's suicide is not the private matter of an individual who decides willfully to part with his life. ⟨...⟩ ⟨H⟩e has agreed to take upon himself the responsibility for the murder of Shatov and thus cover up the criminal activities of Petr Verkhovensky and his collaborators. ⟨...⟩

⟨...⟩ Kirillov claims that he has "no higher idea than disbelief in God.... Man has done nothing but invent God so as to go on living, and not to kill himself.... To recognise that there is no God and not to recognise at the same instant that one is God oneself is an absurdity, else one would certainly kill oneself." ⟨...⟩

On the artistic plane according to V. V. Vinogradov, Dostoevsky's portrayal of Kirillov has been influenced by V. Hugo's "Le dernier jour d'un condamné" ⟨...⟩. The condemned man has a dream in which he finds himself in a dark room with a little old woman. Candle in hand he tries to locate her when suddenly she bites him in the hand. Similarly, Petr Verkhovensky, being in doubt as to Kirillov's final intentions, pursues the invisible Kirillov candle in hand. All of a sudden he becomes aware of a fearful pain in the little finger of his left hand and realizes he has been bitten by the bent-down form of Kirillov. Petr Verkhovensky tears his finger away and rustles headlong out of the house. Vinogradov points out that the nightmarish dream of Hugo's man condemned to death is transformed by Dostoevsky into the literary reality of a pre-death frenzy by a suicide who has condemned himself to death. The motions and the actions of Hugo's mysterious old woman are passed on to Kirillov, but instead of being an expression of the condemned man's anguish, they become part and parcel of the fate of the hero who chooses to die by his own volition.

Biting Petr's finger is Kirillov's last act before he finally shoots himself. It is a symbolic revenge on a man whom he despises and who forces him to commit suicide on terms previously unacceptable to him. Kirillov refuses initially to take responsibility for the crimes perpetrated by Verkhovensky. Finally, by being driven into a frenzy, he signs a note dictated to him by Verkhovensky. Instead of biting Verkhovensky's finger Kirillov could have killed his tormentor before finally putting an end to himself. Such action would be contrary to Kirillov's nature. At one point Verkhovensky suggests that instead of shooting himself, Kirillov could have killed someone else in order to demonstrate his self-will, but Kirillov retorts that "to kill some one would be the lowest point of self-will, and you show your soul in that. I am not you: I want the highest point and I'll kill myself."

E. Wasiolek asserts that Petr's casual remark exposes the deception which is at the core of Kirillov's thinking. Petr shows that the low point of Kirillov's act is just as logical as the high point: "Kirillov believes that with the death of God, man will be free to be good; but the logical consequence is that without God, man will be free to do his pleasure, and neither good nor evil will exist." It appears thus that in his reply to Petr Verkhovensky, Kirillov negates the freedom which he advocates; he brings back the old values from which his suicide is supposed to liberate him. ⟨...⟩

⟨...⟩ Till the very last moment Verkhovensky is not sure whether Kirillov will actually shoot himself or whether Kirillov will attempt to kill him instead. ⟨...⟩

⟨...⟩ Like the existentialists, Dostoevsky stresses in his art the extreme and exceptional experience of man, and his heroes express their freedom of choice in extreme terms. The underground man, and Kirillov who follows him, use their freedom to exemplify the unpredictable character of the universe they confront and to wage metaphysical rebellion against society and against themselves. By killing himself Kirillov exposes the logical implications of total freedom with terrifying clarity, because only death is the absolute proof and irrefutable argument of one's free choice. By his suicide Kirillov endorses everything Albert Camus was later to call "the absurd."

—N. N. Shneidman, *Dostoevsky and Suicide* (Oakville: Mosaic Press, 1984): pp. 56, 57, 58, 61, 62.

RENÉ GIRARD ON MYSHKIN, STAVROGIN, AND THE UNDERGROUND

[René Girard (b. 1923) is the Andrew B. Hammond Professor Emeritus of French Language, Literature, and Civilization at Stanford University. His books include *Deceit, Desire, and the Novel: Self and Other in Literary Structure*

(1965), *Violence and the Sacred* (1977), and *"To Double Business Bound": Essays on Literature, Mimesis, and Anthropology* (1978). Below, he considers the genesis of and interconnections between the figures of Stavrogin and Prince Myshkin.]

⟨...⟩ The two men are antitheses of each other. Both are uprooted aristocrats; both remain outside the frantic agitation that they arouse. Both are masters of the game that they are not concerned to win. But Stavrogin is different from Myshkin in being cruel and insensitive. The suffering of others leaves him indifferent, unless, perhaps, he takes a perverse pleasure in it. He is young, handsome, rich, and intelligent; he has received more than his share of all the gifts that nature and society can confer on an individual. That is why he lives in the most complete boredom: he has no more desires, for he has possessed everything.

Here it is necessary to give up the traditional view that insists on the "autonomy" of the characters in fiction. The notebooks of Dostoevsky demonstrate that Myshkin and Stavrogin have a common origin. These two characters embody contradictory responses, because they are hypothetical responses to one and only one question: the spiritual meaning of detachment. ⟨...⟩

Faced with Myshkin's remarkable success with women, his rival for Aglaya wonders whether the prince is not the most cunning and diabolical of men rather than the simplest. A somewhat similar incident happens in *Demons*. The limping woman, a person half mad but inspired, whom Stavrogin has married out of bravado, at first sees in him the hero and saint who must emerge one day to save Russia. It is therefore possible to ask oneself whether Myshkin is not Stavrogin and, reciprocally, whether Stavrogin is not Myshkin. ⟨...⟩

The project of writing *The Idiot*, conceiving a hero whom his perfection, not his imperfection, separates from others—this is to affirm his own innocence and to transfer all his guilt onto others. Inversely, the project of writing *Demons*, conceiving a hero whose detachment is a form of moral and spiritual degradation—this is to refuse the former kind of justification, to refuse to read any superiority whatever into the lucidity that dismantles and reassembles the dimensions of the underground. The "detachment" does not prove that one has conquered one's own pride; it proves only that one has exchanged slavery for mastery. The roles are reversed but the structure of intersubjective relations remains the same. ⟨...⟩

Stavrogin is to all his satellites what the insolent officer is to the underground man, the unsurpassable obstacle of whom one finally makes an absolute when one wants to be absolute oneself. The theme of the obstacle, like all the underground themes, acquires in *Demons* a quasi-mythical dimension. Stavrogin agrees to hold a duel, or rather, to serve as a target for a man whose father he gravely insulted. He shows such indifference to the bullets of his adversary that the latter, greatly shaken, is not even capable of aiming. This is precisely the mastery of oneself that permits domination of the underground. ⟨...⟩

⟨...⟩ Masochism and sadism constitute the sacraments of the underground mystique. Submitting to suffering reveals to the masochist the nearness of the divine executioner, and inflicting suffering gives the sadist the illusion of embodying this executioner in the exercise of his sacred power. ⟨...⟩

Underground life is a hate-filled imitation of Stavrogin. The latter, whose name means "bearer of the cross," usurps the place of Christ with the ones possessed. With Peter Verkhovensky he forms the Spirit of subversion, and with Stepan Verkhovensky, father of Peter and spiritual father of Stavrogin (he was his tutor), he forms a sort of demoniac counter-trinity. The universe of hate parodies, in the least details, the universe of divine love. Stavrogin and the possessed whom he brings along in his train are all in quest of a wrong-way redemption whose theological name is damnation. ⟨...⟩

—René Girard, *Resurrection from the Underground,* James G. Williams, trans. (New York: Crossroad Publishing, 1997): pp. 81–82, 83, 84, 87, 88, 89.

Plot Summary of
The Brothers Karamazov

Dmitry Merezhkovsky's observation that "A novel of Dostoevsky's is not a tranquil, smoothly developing episode, but a collection of the fifth acts of many tragedies," may nowhere apply with more force than in *The Brothers Karamazov,* his last and grandest work.

The novel opens by introducing us to Fyodor Karamazov and his three legitimate sons: Dmitri, by his first wife; and Ivan and Alyosha by his second wife. Dmitri's mother had eloped with a young seminarian and died in St. Petersburg; Ivan's and Alyosha's mother, driven by her husband to madness, died too. Karamazov then "simply forgets" the children he has fathered, throwing himself wholeheartedly into a life of drunkenness and lechery. Dmitri is adopted by a cousin and leads "a wild life" fighting in the Caucasus: he has, it is clear, inherited his father's sensuality. Ivan, the intellectual son, distinguishes himself at the university and, at 24, has already published an article (about ecclesiastical courts) that provokes considerable commentary. The youngest son, Alyosha, has resolved to join a religious order.

Dmitri confronts Karamazov to demand his mother's inheritance, but is told that the money has all been spent. It is decided that the two should settle their dispute with the help of Zosima, Alyosha's elder. The meeting, however, ends in a quarrel as father and son each accuse the other of trying to buy the favors of the somewhat notorious Grushenka. In the midst of the shouting Zosima suddenly bows and kisses Dmitri's feet, in homage to the great suffering he sees in store for him. "If you ask me," comments the student Rakitin, "he smelled crime. It stinks in your family."

Soon after this the narrator describes the epileptic Smerdyakov, who is employed as Karamazov's servant and who, it is implied (though never decisively confirmed), was fathered by him—probably by force—upon the imbecile Lizaveta.

Alyosha is now accosted by Dmitri, who explains that he has borrowed 3,000 rubles from his fiancée Katerina and spent it on Grushenka. Dmitri wants to be released from the engagement, and begs Alyosha's help to pay Katerina back. Karamazov, meanwhile, has placed 3,000 roubles in an envelope and promises it to Grushenka "if she wants to come." Dmitri, convinced Grushenka has yielded to Karamazov, attacks him, but is restrained by his brothers.

Alyosha, who has failed to persuade Katerina, meets Ivan at a tavern (**Part II**) and they continue the conversation that had been interrupted by Dmitri. Ivan "rebels" against a metaphysical order that rests on the suffering of innocents: "It's not that I don't accept God, Alyosha, I just most respectfully return him the ticket." He completes his case against God in "The Grand Inquisitor," reiterating that "if God is dead, everything is permitted" and declaring that, though he rejects the world, the Karamazov sensuality will keep him living. Dostoevsky's faith was never an easy one, and he published these chapters without knowing if he would be able to refute them with the rest of his novel.

"You go right, I'll go left," Ivan tells Alyosha, sending him back to the monastery. There Zosima is dying, and we are given a sketch of his early life.

It had been expected by many that Zosima's body would not decay (**Part III**). In fact, however, its stench is so overwhelming that many begin to doubt his piety. His faith shaken, Alyosha goes to Grushenka, but her view of the world turns out to be not that of a depraved sensualist, but one in which—as in a fable she relates—a wicked woman might be saved from damnation by an onion. Feeling overwhelmed, Alyosha returns to the monastery, there to recall in a half-dream the wedding at Cana. He awakens in a religious ecstasy, his faith restored, and prepares to obey Zosima's dying injunction: to go out into the world.

Dmitri's many attempts to secure the money have failed, and he resolves to kill himself if he cannot pay back Katerina and "lift from his chest, 'from that place on his chest,' the shame he carried there." He picks up a brass pestle and climbs over a fence into his father's garden. Karamazov is there in the house—but not Grushenka. In his flight Dmitri strikes down the servant Grigory.

Grushenka, Dmitri learns, has gone to Kalganov, the army officer who had abandoned her five years before. Dmitri finds them together at an inn, and offers him three thousand roubles to leave her. She, realizing she loves him, comes back to him, but a contingent of officers soon arrive to arrest Dmitri for his father's murder.

The evidence is circumstantial, but so overwhelming that even Grushenka believes Dmitri a parricide. And here we are finally given Dmitri's account of the events of that night (in the original narrative, the crucial moments had been marked with a line of ellipses). The garden door, he remembers, was shut when he left it, but the police found it open and—as Dmitri himself attests—only he, his father, and Smerdyakov knew the signal. The officers observe that Smerdyakov must then be the murderer, but Dmitri objects on the grounds of both the bastard's cowardice and his lack of motive. Smerdyakov, they tell him, in fact suffered a series of violent epileptic fits on that night. "In that case," bursts out Dmitri, "the devil killed my father!"

Under further interrogation Dmitri finally admits that he had *not* spent the entire three thousand on Grushenka when he fled with her before, but only half of it, wearing the other half in an amulet around his neck. He confesses this with shame: to him the deliberate hoarding of half the money is a "fatal difference," implying a calculation far more debased than would mere impulsive robbery.

The narrator now describes (**Part IV**) the friendship Alyosha has struck up with a group of boys, one of whom, Ilyusha, they had taunted and who is now dying. Smerdyakov, meanwhile, confesses to Ivan that it was he who murdered Karamazov: "You killed him, you are the main killer . . . and I performed the deed according to your word." The truth is as Dmitri had suggested: Smerdyakov could not have committed the crime alone. In a delirium, Ivan is visited and taunted by the devil, his Dostoevskian "double." There is then a sudden knocking at the window and Alyosha arrives—to announce that Smerdyakov has hanged himself.

Ivan has now fallen into a fever, and without his testimony, the case against Dmitri is strong enough to convict him. Especially powerful is the evidence of Katerina, who testifies that Dmitri had contemplated murdering his father. The jury takes only an hour to find Dmitri guilty.

The **Epilogue** ends with Alyosha giving a eulogy for Ilyusha in which he suggests that "even if only one good memory remains with us in our hearts, that alone may serve some day for our salvation." Nathan Rosen observed of Book VI that "'The Russian Monk' is best understood as a two-dimensional icon that has its fourth dimension in the reader's unconscious memories of childhood"; and the same might be said of the novel itself. "The boys are guilty," explains Robin Feuer Miller, "they have all contributed to Ilyusha's suffering. Yet they accept themselves and their brotherhood, though their edifice does stand upon a child's tears." This, finally, is Alyosha's and Zosima's—and Dostoevsky's—answer to Ivan's rebellion: not the denial of our guilt, but its redemption in forgiveness and love. ❦

List of Characters in *The Brothers Karamazov*

Alexei Fyodorovich Karamazov (**Alyosha**) is the protagonist and the youngest of the Karamazov brothers. Gentle and wise, Alyosha is the opposite of his coarse and vulgar father. He decides to join a religious order and enters a monastery, where he becomes a pupil of Zosima.

Dmitri Fyodorovich Karamazov, passionate and intemperate, is the eldest of the Karamazov brothers. He loses interest in his fiancée Katerina and falls in love with Grushenka. Plagued with the burden of sin, he struggles throughout the novel to overcome his flawed nature and to attain spiritual redemption.

Ivan Fyodorovich Karamazov is the second of the Karamazov brothers. As a brilliant student, he demands a logical explanation for everything that occurs in the universe. Consequently, he is plagued by religious doubt and cannot reconcile the idea of suffering with the idea of a loving God. After his forceful arguments about a malevolent God lead to the murder of his father, Ivan is driven to madness.

Fyodor Pavlovich Karamazov is the wealthy head of the Karamazov family and father of Alyosha, Dmitri, Ivan and most likely Smerdyakov. Coarse, vulgar, and lustful, Fyodor is hated by almost everyone who knows him. He lives only to the satisfaction of his senses, giving no thought to those he betrays or hurts. He has no affection for his children, and is eventually murdered by Smerdyakov.

Agrafena Alexandrovna Svetlov (**Grushenka**) is a beautiful young woman who is brought to the town by Samsonov after she is betrayed by a lover. She is the object of desire among the men of the town, and is the source of much animosity between Fyodor and Dmitri. Headstrong and proud, she devotes herself to increasing her wealth by making shrewd investments. Gentleness and love begin to emerge in her character after she meets Alyosha.

Pavel Fyodorovich Smerdyakov is the son of Lizaveta Smerdyashchaya and Fyodor Karamazov. He is raised by Grigory and his wife Marfa, and is made to work in Fyodor's house as a servant. Cursed with epilepsy, Smerdyakov has a mean temperament, but he is very interested in discussing philosophy with Ivan. Ivan's advocacy of religious amorality leads Smerdyakov to murder Fyodor.

Zosima is the wise old elder of the monastery who acts as Alyosha's mentor and teacher. He preaches a message of cherishing God's creation and forgiving the sins of others. Zosima's faith gives him extraordinary insight into the minds of the people he meets.

Katerina Ivanovna Verkhovtsev is Dmitri's fiancée whom he abandons after falling in love with Grushenka. Her anguish over the treatment she receives from Dmitri leads her to adopt an attitude of martyrdom. She humiliates herself by remaining loyal to those who hurt her. Though she loves Ivan, she is unable to act on her love until the end of the novel.

Ilyusha Snegiryov is the son of a military captain who Alyosha befriends. He retains his pride by refusing to cower before the larger boys who pick on him. He falls ill and dies toward the end of the novel, with Alyosha giving the eulogy at his funeral. ❦

Critical Views on
The Brothers Karamazov

R. P. Blackmur on Guilt

[Poet R. P. Blackmur (1904–1965), one of the founders of New Criticism, taught at Princeton University. His books include *The Double Agent: Essays in Craft and Elucidation* (1935), *The Lion and the Honeycomb: Essays in Solicitude and Critique* (1955), and *Form and Value in Modern Poetry* (1957). Here, he explains that Karamazov's murder is a communal crime: "None of them, taken separately, has an adequate motive to murder their father, but taken together in each other's light . . . an ample and powerful sense of motive is achieved. We see now without recognition what we will learn later: that none are guilty and all are guilty."]

⟨. . .⟩ All the brothers have been raised apart, each has been educated as his variation warranted, Dmitri in the army, Ivan at the university, Alyosha at the monastery: old Karamazov in debasement, Smerdyakov in degradation, Dmitri in the pride of body, Ivan in the pride of intellect, Alyosha in a humility which comes close to acting like a pride. With respect to each other, each has passed twenty years in the desert. When they come together, though each is also himself, they unite and break in a single storm on the community. Under the genius of the family they make, as Brutus says in *Julius Caesar*, an insurrection in the state of man. ⟨. . .⟩

Let us look how the thing becomes communal and how in anonymity we find our own name. Old Karamazov ripens his own murder by being himself, by being a buffoon, by taunting his sons, by his sensuality, by his money, by the insult of his creation of Smerdyakov, and by his rivalry with Dmitri over Grushenka. Katerina ripens the murder by her virtue and her pride and fanatic self-humiliation, by her love for Ivan, by tempting Grushenka with kisses, by tempting Dmitri with money, by heightening others' emotions, by eliciting judgment from Alyosha. Ivan ripens the murder by his contempt and pride, by envisaging and suggesting murder, by his *dealing* with Smerdyakov and his father, by his deceit as to where he is going on the fatal day, by his insistence that all things are lawful. Dmitri ripens the murder by comforting

Grushenka and aiding her with relation to the lover who has deserted her, and by his quality as her conscience. Grushenka herself ripens the murder by being "on the market" and by her coquetry. Lastly, Smerdyakov ripens the murder because he is smeared all over; by his appeal to Ivan, the clever man, the appeal of the possibility; by his hatred of the legitimate; by his idiocy, contemplativeness, and epilepsy: that is, by his possibility of bringing together in anonymity the fragments of a general act. He has all the defects of humanity but is incapable of virtues, vices, heroisms. He is smeared and smears, the very thing on the verge. Although, as we know, he "actually" performs the murder, he is the one person who cannot take on himself the guilt of it; the guilt merely demolishes him. We are glad he kills himself, because we could not have established his guilt either.

Why, with all these matters in mind, are we so ready to believe along with every one in the book except Smerdyakov, that it was Dmitri who killed his father? ⟨. . .⟩ Or, to put it another way, why are we prepared (beforehand, from birth) to accept the peasants' verdict—the truesaying—of his guilt beyond above beside the law and the facts? Do we not ourselves occupy *in the shape of Dmitri* the darkness in which the old man was killed? Certainly we cannot so easily choose Ivan's shape or the shape of Ivan's devil; though it is an obvious possibility, it would not be right for the mystery that in the end alone seems live. There is also in the reserve part of our natures the possibility that we might occupy the darkness in the shape of Smerdyakov, just as we might in the uncreated part of our natures occupy it in the shape of Alyosha. We have the epileptic in reserve, who would take us over in his scream, and we have the saint to come, in whom we should disappear. Only in the shape of Dmitri can we participate in a mad but gallant action.

It is in Dmitri that we can accommodate ourselves to the Elder Zossima, to the Grand Inquisitor, and to the sweep or momentum of the story. And it is in Dmitri that we can believe for the length of the story that all are guilty and that none are guilty. Each of us can strike himself, as Dmitri did, "here," on the breast. ⟨. . .⟩

—R. P. Blackmur, *Eleven Essays in the European Novel* (New York: Harcourt, Brace & World, 1964): pp. 188, 198–99.

Robert L. Belknap on the Narrative

[Robert L. Belknap is Professor Emeritus of Slavic Languages at Columbia University. He has written *Tradition and Innovation: General Education and the Reintegration of the University* (with Richard Kuhns, 1977) and *The Genesis of* The Brothers Karamazov (1992), and edited *Russianness: Studies on a Nation's Identity: In Honor of Rufus Mathewson, 1918–1978* (1990). Here, Belknap shows how the narrator achieves a hallucinatory effect by bending and reversing time. He further considers *Karamazov* both as psychological novel and as allegory.]

This delay in the operation of grace is a central theme of the novel. The whole imagery of seeds in the earth is united with this causal mechanism by the epigraph of the novel: "Except a grain of wheat fall upon the ground and die, it abideth alone, but if it die, it bringeth forth much fruit." The novel can be looked at as the record of the action of grace upon a group of people. The delay in Zosima and Alëša is the period in which the seed of grace dies, admitting that sense of guilt which seems to be necessary if grace is to be communicable, bearing fruit. Mitja's insemination with grace comes in the obeisances of Zosima and Katja or maybe Dr. Herzenstube's gift of nuts, but the fruit does not come until his dream of the babe. Ivan's insemination with grace comes from his mother, and from Alëša, in the kiss that plagiarizes Christ in the Legend of the Grand Inquisitor. For Ivan, this redemption is not complete. ⟨...⟩

Chronological order may be reversed, so that people respond to what has not yet happened, as the White Queen screams before cutting her finger.[6] ⟨...⟩ Ivan's malaise after the Legend is due to his forthcoming encounter with Smerdjakov. Smerdjakov's fake fit is followed by a real one. Zosima bows down before Mitja because of what is going to happen to him. Alëša blushes before the *nadryv* at Katerina Ivanovna's, and he trembles before the *nadryv* with Snegirëv. Mitja offers an extreme case of such causation when he suggests that Alëša had arrived because Mitja was thinking about him. ⟨...⟩

All these distortions in time and in the causal pattern disturb readers by illustrating one of the more difficult teachings of Zosima's brother, Markel: "Like the ocean, all things flow and touch together; you push in one place, and it gives at the other end of the world."

(IX, 400) In the causal structure of the novel, Dostoevskij practices the unity of the universe which he preaches in the words of Zosima and Markel. ⟨...⟩

The manipulation of the narrator's awareness has a more interesting effect on the reader's apprehension of other characters. When the reasons and desires, doubts and regrets of a character are shown in relation to the world about him, he becomes a humanly motivated, psychologically understandable being, his humanity exceeding his goodness or badness or any other quality. But when a character is seen only from the outside, especially when his actions are obscurely or complicatedly related to the outer world, the reader tends to remember him not as a person, but as a token of some force or quality transcending humanity. ⟨...⟩

During the first day covered by the novel, Mitja is treated externally, tending to become the personification of the violent Karamazov sensuality. During the second and third days, the time covered by Book Eight, he is treated with insight into his state of mind and becomes a desperate human being. I have already alluded to the Hell of jealousy, desperation, hate, fumes, frustration, blood, despair, delirium, and guilt through which Mitja passes, and to the purgatory of his questioning, which is so labeled in the chapter headings. At the end of this purgatory, Mitja dreams of the weeping babe and wakes having passed the turning point towards Zosima's heaven on earth, as his words then and thereafter show. At this point the primary narrator loses insight into Mitja's mind. ⟨...⟩

This coexistence of two kinds of narrative awareness, often in the same scene, as with Ivan and Smerdjakov, and sometimes with the same character, as with Alëša, produces the spontaneous apprehension of two levels of existence. ⟨...⟩ It is not hard to say that Alëša Karamazov is sometimes himself and sometimes Christ, but when these two natures are enacted not only in his own behavior and relationships, but in the medium through which he is known, the reader has a disquietingly compelling sense that this intellectual talk has become urgent fact. ⟨...⟩

Note
⁶ Lewis Carroll, *The Complete Works of Lewis Carroll* (New York, undated), p. 198.

—Robert L. Belknap, *The Structure of* The Brothers Karamazov (The Hague: Mouton, 1967): pp. 74, 86–88.

RICHARD PEACE ON DMITRI'S PUNISHMENT

[Richard Peace has taught at Bristol University, and is the author of *The Enigma of Gogol: An Examination of the Writings of N. V. Gogol and Their Place in the Russian Literary Tradition* (1981), *Chekhov: A Study of the Four Major Plays* (1983), and *Oblomov: A Critical Examination of Goncharov's Novel* (1991). At their meeting in Zosima's cell, the monk offers Ivan his blessing, but bows down to Dmitri. In this extract, Peace explains why.]

The devil cannot resolve Ivan's doubts; he can only exacerbate them; for the devil is only Ivan himself, or rather one part of him—he is Ivan's intellect mirroring itself in destructive self-mockery.

At the same time, however, the devil is also a manifestation of a non-rational function of Ivan's mind—conscience; for this hallucination is symptomatic of a growing inner awareness of his own complicity in the death of his father. That this instrument of conscience should be a mirror mocking his intellect is only just, since the guilt of Ivan is the guilt of the intellect. It is fitting too that its outward form should be seen to resemble that of the devil; for, as we have seen in the last chapter, the crime of Ivan is in essence theological parricide. ⟨...⟩

Zosima makes his obeisance to Dmitri because he senses that Dmitri will undergo both forms of punishment of which he himself had been speaking shortly before. The following day, on the eve of his death, he offers an explanation of his action: 'I bowed down yesterday to the great suffering that awaits him in the future.' This in itself, of course, is not absolutely explicit, but it must be taken in conjunction with the highly significant terminology in which Zosima had chosen to couch his disquisition on punishment. The word here used for 'punishment' is not *nakazaniye* (the word which figures in the title: *Crime and Punishment*) it is *kara* [punishment, retribution] and when this word next occurs in the novel, it is during the trial of Dmitri. ⟨...⟩

The word '*kara*', therefore, seems to be particularly associated with Dmitri. He is 'Karamazov'—'punishment-daubed' (the second element of his surname, '*maz*' suggests '*mazat*'—'to daub', 'to smear'). It is, of course, a name which he shares in common with his brothers and his father; they too, in their different ways, undergo punishment, but it is in Dmitri that the full implications of *kara* are worked out. ⟨...⟩

The dream ⟨...⟩ is an expression of Dmitri's parricidal guilt, and it is significant that it reproduces elements of his 'plunge into the abyss beneath his feet'—that mad ride to Mokroye. On that occasion the evidence of Dmitri's parricidal guilt had appeared overwhelming. ⟨...⟩

It is after the three infernal 'ordeals' of the preliminary investigation that Dmitri has his revealing dream, and in it are reproduced the fast ride, the questions to the coachman, and above all the figure of the child—the child whose plight Dmitri cannot understand; for in spite of the assurances of Andrey, the child has suffered an ordeal of fire. It is this image of the child which haunts Dmitri and will influence the whole of his future life: ⟨...⟩

> ⟨...⟩ All people are 'bairns'. I shall go for them all, because it is necessary for someone to go for all. (Bk xi, Ch. 4)

The plight of the child demands sacrifice; Dmitri is going to accept suffering for all. In this he is a Christ-figure, and it is therefore not surprising that it is Christ's prophecy of his own death and resurrection (St John xii. 24) which serves as an epigraph for the whole novel, and is applied more particularly to the fate of Dmitri. Thus Zosima quotes this passage of Scripture to Alesha in explaining the reason for his obeisance to Dmitri. The quotation occurs again in Zosima's testament, where it is a turning point in the account of his relations with 'the mysterious visitor'; a story which is a parable about the terrible power of conscience, and as such sheds light on the inner torments of both Dmitri and Ivan.

—Richard Peace, *Dostoyevsky: An Examination of the Major Novels* (Cambridge: Cambridge University Press, 1971): pp. 279, 280–81, 282, 284–85.

Malcolm V. Jones on the Grand Inquisitor

[Malcolm V. Jones is Professor of Russian and Slavonic Studies at Nottingham University. He is the author of *Dostoyevsky After Bakhtin: Readings in Dostoyevsky's Fantastic Realism* (1990), and editor of *New Essays on Tolstoy* (1978), *Dostoevsky and the Twentieth Century: The Ljubljana Papers*

(1993), and *The Cambridge Companion to the Classic Russian Novel* (with Robin Feuer Miller, 1998). Here he explains that "[l]ike other of Dostoyevsky's heroes, Ivan has an ideal picture of Christ, but has no sense of his identity with a loving Creator"—and shows that this in turn is true also of Ivan's own "poetic" invention, the Grand Inquisitor.]

⟨. . .⟩ He is not infrequently called an atheist, and he does indeed express the view that God does not exist. ⟨. . .⟩ ⟨I⟩n his confession to Alyosha Ivan declares that he accepts God; it is simply his world that he does not accept. If this is the 'real' Ivan it would seem misplaced to call him either an atheist or an agnostic; he would seem rather to be a believer, in revolt against his Creator. The title of the chapter ('Rebellion'), in which Ivan makes his protest, might seem to lend weight to such a conclusion. Undoubtedly Ivan is at his most direct and sincere in this last mood; some readers have seen evidence of gnostic ideas in his declaration.

It is worth mentioning this divergence of opinions because the case is often not carefully argued. Ivan is merely assumed to be one of the three. But when all is said and done, the truth is that Ivan is confused about the existence of God. ⟨. . .⟩ His fundamental conclusion is that if there is no immortality and God does not exist then there is no basis for virtue. If he does exist, it is implied, then he cannot be the sort of God from whom principles of virtue can be derived. If that is the case, then cannibalism is the only sane, rational principle on which to base one's behaviour. Raskolnikov's dream in Siberia, Ippolit's intuition of ultimate reality, now find theoretical justification. ⟨. . .⟩

It has to be emphasised that the Grand Inquisitor, whatever may be true of Ivan, is an atheist, and this fundamentally influences his understanding of Christ and of Christianity. Christ's appearance to him has much the same ambiguity as that of the devil to Ivan. Ivan makes it clear, as the narrator does in the case of Ivan's devil, that the whole thing may have been an hallucination. The Inquisitor, to judge from, his tone regards Christ as his equal if not his inferior. The fact that he recognises him as Christ cannot be taken as evidence that he acknowledges him as the Son of God any more than Ivan acknowledges the objective existence of the devil. The significant thing is that God does not come into the picture at all and particularly not as a loving God, taking the initiative in seeking men before they seek him, infinitely merciful and redemptive. Indeed the conception of a God of Grace sustaining the Church and its members through the Holy Spirit is most conspicuously absent, for Christianity has never claimed that men in their weakness are strong enough to shoulder the burden of freedom *alone*. Christianity preaches the very opposite: that they are not, not even Grand Inquisitors. ⟨...⟩

Some commentators have ⟨...⟩ seen signs of Divine grace in the impact which the Inquisitor's Christ has on the crowds who recognise him as he walks through the streets of Seville. This is only significant for the total view of the world represented in the Legend if it be assumed beyond doubt that this Christ is real. But Ivan himself does not encourage such a view. In answer to Alyosha, he says:

> 'Take the latter alternative,' laughed Ivan, 'if contemporary realism has so spoilt you that you can't accept anything fantastic. If you want a *quid pro quo,* so be it. It is true,' he laughed again, 'the old man is ninety, and he could quite well have gone out of his mind long ago about his idea. The prisoner's appearance might have struck him. It might, after all, have been simply delirium, the vision of a ninety-year-old man before his death, his mind still in a fever as a result of the burning of a hundred heretics the day before. But what does it matter to us whether it was a *quid pro quo* or a wild fantasy? The only thing that matters is that the old man had to speak out, that, finally he does speak out for all his ninety years, and he says aloud what for ninety years he has kept silent about.'

As Ivan says, what matters is the confession of the Grand Inquisitor, the thoughts which have been accumulating within him for a lifetime, and *his* image of Christ.

—Malcolm V. Jones, *Dostoyevsky: The Novel of Discord* (London: Paul Elek, 1976): pp. 178–79, 183, 185.

Robert Louis Jackson on Ivan's Rebellion

[Robert Louis Jackson is the B. E. Bensinger Professor Emeritus of Slavic Languages and Literatures at Yale University. His books include *Dostoevsky's Underground Man in Russian Literature* (1958), *Dostoevsky's Quest for Form: A Study of His Philosophy of Art* (1966), and *Dialogues with Dostoevsky: The Overwhelming Questions* (1993). Below, he considers the theme of lamentation, first raised in the chapter "Women with Faith" (where the narrator remarks that "Such grief . . . does not desire consolation"), and reveals its centrality to Ivan's repudiation of God.]

The center of Ivan's lamentation, literally and figuratively, is a wound, an image paralyzing to mind and spirit: it is the mutilation, the physical as well as psychological disfiguration, of children. Zosima envisages the departed child rejoicing in his resurrected state over his mother's tears and pointing them out to God. ⟨. . .⟩ ⟨I⟩mmortality renders inconsolable grief meaningless. Ivan, on the other hand, is unable to conjure up visions of angelic children gamboling about the throne of God the Father and rejoicing at the tears of their grief-stricken mothers on earth. Ivan has other visions the contemplation of which lead him neither to quiet emotion, nor to spiritual catharsis, nor to a feeling of absolution for his sins. ⟨. . .⟩

The various images that appear in Ivan's peroration are, like his stories, lacerations. Ivan's conception of himself as a bedbug, for instance, accurately conveys the hostile, underground character of his pose of humility: "I am a bedbug, and I confess with all humility that I cannot understand anything, why everything is arranged as it is." The whole movement of Ivan's monologue—viewed as antitheodicy—is a steady ascent from earth to heaven, from bedbug to God. The ascent is steep and ends in a reversal of roles: the humiliation of God, the representation of Him as a scurrilous merchandizer of souls, and the transformation of the bedbug, Ivan, into a Christ figure. ⟨. . .⟩

⟨. . .⟩ The god against whom Ivan rebels is conceived as a supreme merchant or pawnbroker, trafficking in the sufferings of mankind and selling "tickets" to heaven at exorbitant rates of interest. Ivan pursues the metaphor with a vengeance. In his conception, man must "buy" (*kupit', pokupat'*) eternal harmony with suffering, but at an unfavorable exchange rate. ⟨...⟩

In the ironic subtext of Ivan's rebellious lamentation, Jesus the Redeemer (the only being, Ivan hints, who might have the "right to forgive") stands opposed to God the merchant. Jesus does not appear in Ivan's lamentation, but his omission is deliberate. Jesus has not yet arrived in the cruel Old Testament world that Ivan posits. He is only an hypothesis in Ivan's legend of the Grand Inquisitor, as he is in the long tirade where Ivan allows that "in the world's finale, at the moment of eternal harmony, something so precious [might] come to pass that it would suffice for all hearts, for the assuaging of all resentments, for the expiation of all the crimes of humanity ... that it will make it not only possible to forgive but to justify all that has happened with men." ⟨...⟩

⟨...⟩ Both pictures are constructed out of contradictory emotional elements. But in Ivan's picture the contradiction is, as it were, malignant: the jarring elements constitute a permanent laceration; the idea of a reconciliation between the general and the mother is perceived, literally and figuratively, as both impossible and repulsive. In Zosima's picture, on the other hand, the jarring elements (the tears of the mother and the laughter of the child) are resolved in the triumphant miracle of resurrection. In Ivan's picture the owner of the dogs, the general, is a satanic figure; the mother, in effect, embraces the devil. In Zosima's picture, the satanic figure is replaced by an unseen but ever-present and solicitous God. ⟨...⟩

⟨...⟩ Psychologically, Ivan's choice of endless suffering is embodied in his rebellious lamentation. It can be compared to the Underground Man's revolt against the laws of nature or the "stone wall": it is neither victory nor reconciliation, but, figuratively speaking, a permanent, despairing beating of the head against the wall. ⟨...⟩

⟨...⟩ Konstantin Mochulsky has called attention to the element of "imposture" in Ivan's rebellion: "A diabolic deceit is hidden in this imposture. The atheist appeals to the noble human sentiments of compassion, magnanimity, love, but on his lips this is pure rhetoric." Yet it seems there is more than diabolic deceit and conceit here. The very nature of Ivan's imposture is deeply ambivalent. What he sets out to deny, he affirms in spite of himself by his unconscious wish to imitate Christ. ⟨...⟩

—Robert Louis Jackson, *The Art of Dostoevsky: Deliriums and Nocturnes* (Princeton: Princeton University Press, 1981): pp. 322, 324–25, 328–29, 330, 333–34.

Valentina A. Vetlovskaya on Alyosha

[In this extract, Valentina A. Vetlovskaya examines the relationship of Alyosha and his story to the tradition of the hagiographic hero, specifically the figure of Aleksey the Man of God.]

The basic features of the *vita* of Aleksey the Man of God and of the sacred poem about him are Aleksey's departure from home to perform the exploits customary for the hero of a *vita*, and his life in his parents' home upon his return. ⟨...⟩

⟨...⟩ Alyosha's meeting with his father, then with the schoolchildren, then the "lacerations," of which the gravest is the last (the confession of Captain Snegiryov, in which the theme of the innocently suffering child is heard), continues the grave series of "temptations" of Alyosha. The gloomy impressions from his first days of acquaintance with the world, even before the conversation with his brother Ivan, ⟨...⟩ make Alyosha let slip a phrase expressing something that was "already undoubtedly tormenting him": "And perhaps I don't even believe in God."

Alyosha's sudden confession, on the one hand, and Father Paisy's warning, on the other, uttered on the same day as the brothers' meeting in the tavern, both have a very direct relation to that meeting. Ivan's tempting speech, which comes along with the other temptations but is stronger than they are, is addressed to the hero, who is already disturbed by the world's "darkness." ⟨...⟩

Fulfilling others' requests, listening to others (above all his brother Ivan), Alyosha gives way to temptation. The "darkness" of the world does not remain alien to this hero's heart, and not only because he is too young, but also because Alyosha, as he himself explains more than once, is a Karamazov. Notwithstanding his strangeness, Alyosha is the same sort of man as everyone else (in contrast to the *vita* and the poem, in the novel this motif is carried out quite definitely). ⟨...⟩

⟨...⟩ Alyosha loved his spiritual father, Father Zosima, too much: "The fact is that all the love that lay concealed in his pure young heart for everyone and everything had, for the past year, been concentrated—and perhaps wrongly so—on one being, now deceased. It is true that that being had for so long been accepted by him as his ideal, that all his young strength and energy could not but turn towards that ideal, even to the forgetting at the moment of everyone and everything." ⟨...⟩

If Alyosha had loved the elder more "correctly," that is, not with an exceptional love but in the same way that he loved others, he would not have found grounds in the righteous man's "shame" for the condemnation of "God's world." Everything in this world is connected. And just as there are none who are completely righteous, so there are none who are completely sinful. For this reason the scene of Alyosha and Grushenka, coming after the scene of the young hero's bitter suffering, harmoniously complements the story about the righteous man's "shame." Here the sinful woman unexpectedly reveals a degree of love, reverence for sanctity, and compassion for her dispirited brother that, considering her "incorrect" view of things, would not be supposed of her. ⟨...⟩

Alyosha's dream ("Cana of Galilee") naturally concludes these scenes. The boundlessness of God's love for all people and the joy of those who are united by this love are manifested here to the young ascetic as if before his very eyes. The link of everyone with each other, salutary and joyful when God is among people ⟨...⟩ staggers Alyosha's soul with ecstasy. The idea of the primordial beauty and purity of "God's world," and of the responsibility of all people for the fact that they make this beautiful world vicious, is what the author tries to emphasize in "Cana of Galilee." It is just this idea that Alyosha suddenly grasps, "for the rest of his life and forever and ever": "What was he weeping over? Oh! in his rapture he was weeping even over those stars, which were shining to him from the abyss of space ... He longed to forgive everyone and for everything, and to beg forgiveness. Oh, not for himself, but for all men, for all and for everything." ⟨...⟩

⟨. . .⟩ Alyosha (not intellectually, but emotionally) finds a way out of suffering in the joyful acceptance of "God's world," and in union with everything and everyone. This loving union with people, the intimate inclusion of them all (including the most sinful) in his soul eliminates the contradiction between love of God and love of people—the basic contradiction overcome by the hero of the ancient *vita*, Aleksey the Man of God. ⟨. . .⟩

—Valentina A. Vetlovskaya, "Alyosha Karamazov and the Hagiographic Hero," *Dostoevsky: New Perspectives*, Robert Louis Jackson, ed. (Englewood Cliffs: Prentice-Hall, 1984): pp. 219, 221, 222–23, 224–25.

ROGER B. ANDERSON ON ZOSIMA AND KARAMAZOV

[Roger B. Anderson's books include *N. M. Karamzin's Prose: The Teller in the Tale, a Study in Narrative Technique* (1974), *Soviet-American Relations: Understanding Differences, Avoiding Conflicts* (co-edited with Daniel N. Nelson, 1988), and *Russian Narrative and Visual Art: Varieties of Seeing* (co-edited with Paul Debreczeny, 1994). In this extract, Anderson suggests that Zosima's teachings are more closely related to myth than to orthodox Christianity. He also compares the figure of the monk with that of the novel's other influential "father," Fyodor Karamazov, in the context of Bakhtinian "carnival."]

The decomposition of Zosima's body upon his death re-creates precisely what nature does each autumn (the time of year of the elder's death). He not only decomposes in physical terms but, like Markel, "fertilizes" the lives of those who follow him (especially Alyosha). What we have, then, are three generations of human life (Markel, Zosima, and Alyosha), each linked to the same spiritual archetypes. The implication is clear that there is no end to the spiritual energy that flows through each. It does not die any more than nature dies at the end of its yearly cycle. ⟨. . .⟩

⟨. . .⟩ Nature is the locus of idealized integration and transformation on an unending basis. It is perpetually both the womb of life and its grave. ⟨. . .⟩

Fyodor and Zosima are, each in his own way, pantheistic. Fyodor's pantheism is reflected in his limitless pagan sexuality, his total devotion of life's energy to sensual experience. No woman is unattractive to him, as he says in "Over Cognac." Each conquest is treasured and unique. Sex for him is a way of immersing himself in nature; he unites with it and draws from it an enormous amount of energy, which he uses in the pursuit of still more sensual experience. ⟨...⟩

Zosima's devotion to nature is also archaic, energetic, and pantheistic. Rocks, trees, grass, birds, and especially the earth are all sources of extraordinary experience for him. Human participation in nature is a cosmic mystery. Zosima shares with Fyodor an undifferentiated sense of life that charges each aspect of nature and human experience with transcendent meaning. All life for him is spiritually valuable, just as all life is filled with sensual value for Fyodor. The "sensual mysticism" that Fedotov ascribes to Russian folk belief fits not only Zosima; it is only a hair's breadth away from the "mystical sensualism" that dominates Fyodor's life. ⟨...⟩

As with Fyodor, Zosima's life before the novel opens is marked by irregularity and several reversals of basic social codes. Zosima threatens the honor of his regiment by throwing his pistol away during a duel. He bows down to an orderly, proclaiming that he would be a servant to his servant. Later, he is associated with the secret murderer whom society wrongly considers a paragon of conventional virtue. Zosima's influence on that murderer appears dangerous to the man's wife and friends, and they link the monk to the man's failing health. In fact, the opposite is true, for illness and contact with Zosima coincide with the murderer's soul-saving public confession. Zosima's behavior is thus consistently misunderstood, and society suspects and resents him as a bad influence on others. The elder's variances from the accepted beliefs of his church have a scandalous effect on monastic society similar to the effect of Fyodor's behavior on the town.

Father Zosima and Fyodor Karamazov represent a kind of open door through which ordinary people vicariously glimpse the mysteries of unbounded, unconventional experience. As literary refractions of the ancient carnival, they both accommodate the mixture and inversion of very different levels of life, levels that society ordinarily strives to keep separate. For each elder, human life blends with nature in transcendent mystery. A Myusov or a Mrs. Khokhlakov, or even the typical monk, cannot accept such a volatile synthesis for themselves, and they seek to suppress it in the irregular Zosima and Fyodor as well. But resistance to unbounded experience for themselves does not dampen their fascination with the extraordinary figures who can enter such a realm. On the contrary, town and monastery are tantalized by these aberrant men.

—Roger B. Anderson, *Dostoevsky: Myths of Duality* (Gainesville: University of Florida Press, 1986): pp. 127, 141, 142, 143–44.

Works by Fyodor Dostoevsky

Eugénie Grandet (Honoré de Balzac), 1844 [translation]

Poor Folk, 1846

The Double, 1846

"Mr. Prokharchin," 1846

"A Novel in Nine Letters," 1847

"The Landlady," 1847

"Another Man's Wife; or, The Husband Under the Bed," 1848

"A Faint Heart," 1848

"Polzunkov," 1848

"Out of the Service," 1848

"An Honest Thief," 1848

"A Christmas Tree and a Wedding," 1848

"White Nights," 1848

Netochka Nezvanova, 1849

"The Little Hero," 1857

"Uncle's Dream," 1859

"The Village of Stepanchikovo" ["The Friend of the Family"], 1859

The Insulted and Injured, 1861

The House of the Dead, 1862

"A Nasty Story," 1862

Winter Notes on Summer Impressions, 1863

Notes from the Underground, 1864

"The Crocodile," 1865

Crime and Punishment, 1866

The Gambler, 1867

The Idiot, 1868

The Eternal Husband, 1870

Demons [The Possessed], 1872

"Bobok," 1873

A Raw Youth [The Adolescent], 1875

"The Peasant Marey," 1876

"The Heavenly Christmas Tree," 1876

"A Gentle Creature," 1876

The Diary of a Writer, 1876

"The Dream of a Ridiculous Man," 1877

The Brothers Karamazov, 1880

"The Pushkin Address," 1880

Works About Fyodor Dostoevsky

Anderson, Nancy K. *The Perverted Ideal in Dostoevsky's* The Devils. New York: Peter Lang, 1997.

Bakhtin, Mikhail. *Problems of Dostoevsky's Poetics.* Trans. R. W. Rotsel. Ann Arbor: Ardis, 1973.

Belknap, Robert L. "The Rhetoric of an Ideological Novel." *Literature and Society in Imperial Russia, 1800–1914,* ed. William Mills Todd III, 197–223. Stanford: Stanford University Press, 1978.

———. *The Structure of* The Brothers Karamazov. The Hague: Mouton, 1967.

Berdyaev, Nicholas. *Dostoevsky.* Trans. Donald Attwater. New York: Meridien, 1960.

Braun, Maximilian. "*The Brothers Karamazov* as an Expository Novel." *Canadian-American Slavic Studies* 6.2 (1972): 199–208.

Busch, R. L. *Humor in the Major Novels of F. M. Dostoevsky.* Columbus: Slavica, 1987.

Catteau, Jacques. *Dostoyevsky and the Process of Literary Creation.* Trans. Audrey Littlewood. Cambridge: Cambridge University Press, 1989.

Cerny, Vaclav. *Dostoevsky and His Devils.* Trans. F. W. Galan. Ann Arbor: Ardis, 1975.

Cox, Gary. *Tyrant and Victim in Dostoevsky.* Columbus: Slavica, 1983.

Dalton, Elizabeth. *Unconscious Structure in* The Idiot: *A Study in Literature and Psychoanalysis.* Princeton: Princeton University Press, 1979.

Davidson, R. M. "*The Devils:* The Role of Stavrogin." *New Essays on Dostoyevsky,* eds. Malcolm V. Jones and Garth M. Terry, 95–114. Cambridge: Cambridge University Press, 1983.

Dostoevsky, Fyodor. *The Notebooks for* The Idiot. Ed. Edward Wasiolek. Chicago: University of Chicago Press, 1967.

Fanger, Donald. *Dostoevsky and Romantic Realism: A Study of Dostoevsky in Relation to Balzac, Dickens, and Gogol.* Cambridge: Harvard University Press, 1965.

Frank, Joseph. *Dostoevsky: The Mantle of the Prophet, 1871–1881.* Princeton: Princeton University Press, 2002.

———. Dostoevsky: *The Miraculous Years, 1865–1871.* Princeton: Princeton University Press, 1995.

Girard, René. *Deceit, Desire, and the Novel: Self and Other in Literary Structure.* Trans. Yvonne Freccero. Baltimore: Johns Hopkins Press, 1965.

Guardini, Romano. "Dostoyevsky's Idiot, A Symbol of Christ." Trans. Francis X. Quinn. *Cross Currents* 6.4 (1956): 359–82.

Ivanov, Vyacheslav. *Freedom and the Tragic Life: A Study in Dostoevsky.* Trans. Norman Cameron. London: Harvill Press, 1952.

Gill, Richard. "The Bridges of St. Petersburg: A Motif in Crime and Punishment." *Dostoevsky Studies* 3 (1982): 145–55.

Guerard, Albert J. "On the Composition of Dostoevsky's *The Idiot.*" *Mosaic* 8.1 (1974): 200–15.

Holquist, Michael. *Dostoevsky and the Novel.* Princeton: Princeton University Press, 1977.

Jones, John. *Dostoevsky.* Oxford: Clarendon Press, 1983.

Kurrick, Maire Jaanus. *Literature and Negation.* New York: Columbia University Press, 1979.

Leatherbarrow, W. J., ed. *Dostoevsky's* The Devils: *A Critical Companion.* Evanston: Northwestern University Press, 1999.

Matlaw, Ralph E. "The Chronicler of *The Possessed:* Character and Function." *Dostoevsky Studies* 5 (1984): 37–47.

Matlaw, Ralph E. "Recurrent Imagery in Dostoevskij." *Harvard Slavic Studies* 3 (1957): 201–25.

Meijer, J. M. "Situation Rhyme in a Novel of Dostoevskij." *Dutch Contributions to the Fourth International Congress of Slavicists,* Moscow, September 1958, 115–29. The Hague: Mouton, 1958.

Miller, Robin Feuer. "The Role of the Reader in *The Idiot.*" *Slavic and East European Journal* 23.2 (1979): 190–202.

Mochulsky, Konstantin. *Dostoevsky: His Life and Work.* Trans. Michael A. Minihan. Princeton: Princeton University Press, 1967.

Morson, Gary Saul. "Verbal Pollution in *The Brothers Karamazov*." *PTL: A Journal for Descriptive Poetics and Theory of Literature* 3 (1978): 25–44.

Nuttall, A. D. Crime and Punishment: *Murder as Philosophic Experiment*. Edinburgh: Sussex University Press, 1978.

Passage, Charles E. *Character Names in Dostoevsky's Fiction*. Ann Arbor: Ardis, 1982.

Peace, Richard. *Dostoyevsky: An Examination of the Major Novels*. Cambridge: Cambridge University Press, 1971.

Proffer, Carl R. *The Unpublished Dostoevsky: Diaries and Notebooks (1860–81)*. 3 vols. Trans. T. S. Berczynski, Barbara Heldt Monter, Arline Boyer, and Ellendea Proffer. Ann Arbor: Ardis, 1973.

Rahv, Philip. *Essays on Literature and Politics, 1932–1972*. Eds. Arabel J. Porter and Andrew J. Dvosin. Boston: Houghton Mifflin, 1978.

Rosen, Nathan. "Style and Structure in *The Brothers Karamazov:* The Grand Inquisitor and the Russian Monk." *Russian Literature Triquarterly* 1 (1971): 352–65.

———. "Why Dmitrii Karamazov Did Not Kill His Father." *Canadian-American Slavic Studies* 6.2 (1972): 209–24.

Rosenshield, Gary. Crime and Punishment: *The Techniques of the Omniscient Author*. Lisse: Peter de Ridder, 1978.

Sandoz, Ellis. *Political Apocalypse: A Study of Dostoevsky's Grand Inquisitor*. Baton Rouge: Louisiana State University Press, 1971.

Seduro, Vladimir. *Dostoyevsky in Russian Literary Criticism 1846–1956*. New York: Columbia University Press, 1957.

Simmons, Ernest J. Dostoevsky: *The Making of a Novelist*. London: John Lehmann, 1950.

Terras, Victor. *A Karamazov Companion*. Madison: University of Wisconsin Press, 1981.

Vivas, Eliseo. "The Two Dimensions of Reality in *The Brothers Karamazov*." *Sewanee Review* 59 (1951): 23–49.

Wasiolek, Edward, ed. Crime and Punishment *and the Critics*. San Francisco: Wadsworth, 1961.

Wasiolek, Edward. *Dostoevsky: The Major Fiction*. Cambridge: MIT Press, 1964.

Welch, Lois M. "Luzhin's Crime and the Advantages of Melodrama in Dostoevsky's *Crime and Punishment.*" *Texas Studies in Literature and Language* 18 (1976): 135–46.

Wellek, René. *Dostoevsky: A Collection of Critical Essays.* Englewood Cliffs: Prentice-Hall, 1962.

Wharton, Robert V. "Dostoevsky's Defense of Christ in *The Brothers Karamazov:* Part Two." *Cithara* 24.1 (1984): 59–70.

———. "Roads to Happiness in *The Brothers Karamazov:* Dostoevsky's Defense of Christ." *Cithara* 23.2 (1984): 3–15.

Acknowledgments

"Traditional Symbolism in *Crime and Punishment*" by George Gibian. From *Publications of the Modern Language Association of America* LXX, no. 5 (1955). © 1955 by the Modern Language Association of America. Reprinted by permission of the Modern Language Association of America.

"On the Structure of *Crime and Punishment*" by Edward Wasiolek. From *Publications of the Modern Language Association of America* LXXIV, no. 1 (1959). © 1959 by the Modern Language Association of America. Reprinted by permission of the Modern Language Association of America.

"Crime for Punishment: The Tenor of Part One" by W. D. Snodgrass. From *The Hudson Review* XIII, no. 2 (1960). © 1960 by *The Hudson Review*. Reprinted by permission of *The Hudson Review*.

"Looking Over Raskol'nikov's Shoulder: The Narrator in 'Crime and Punishment'" by Pierre R. Hart. From *Criticism* XIII, no. 2 (1971). © 1971 by *Criticism*. Reprinted by permission.

"Dostoevskian Patterned Antinomy and Its Function in *Crime and Punishment*" by W. Woodin Rowe. From *Slavic and East European Journal* XVI, no. 3 (1972). © 1972 by *Slavic and East European Journal*. Reprinted by permission.

Problems of Dostoevsky's Poetics by Mikhail Bakhtin, R. W. Rotsel, trans. (Ann Arbor: Ardis, 1973). © 1973 by Ardis Publishers. Reprinted by permission.

"Raskolnikov and the 'Enigma of his Personality'" by W. J. Leatherbarrow. From *Forum for Modern Language Studies* IX, no. 2 (1973). © 1973 by Modern Language Studies. Reprinted by permission of Modern Language Studies.

Crime and Punishment: Murder as Philosophic Experiment by A. D. Nuttall. (Edinburgh: Sussex University Press, 1978). © 1978 by Sussex University Press. Reprinted by permission.

"Dostoyevsky's Women" by F. F. Seeley. From *The Slavonic and East European Review* XXXIX, no. 93 (1961). © 1961 by *The Slavonic and East European Review*. Reprinted by permission.

Between Earth and Heaven: Shakespeare, Dostoevsky, and the Meaning of Christian Tragedy by Roger L. Cox, © 1969 by Roger L. Cox. Reprinted by permission of Henry Holt and Company, LLC.

Holquist, Michael. *Dostoevsky and the Novel.* Copyright © 1977 by Princeton University Press. Reprinted by permission of Princeton University Press.

Dalton, Elizabeth. *Unconscious Structure in* The Idiot: *A Study in Literature and Psychoanalysis.* Copyright © 1979 by Princeton University Press. Reprinted by permission of Princeton University Press.

"Dostoevsky and Politics: Notes on 'The Possessed'" by Philip Rahv. From *Partisan Review* V, no. 2 (1938). © 1938 by Philip Rahv. Reprinted by permission.

Freedom and the Tragic Life: A Study in Dostoevsky by Vyacheslav Ivanov, trans. Norman Cameron (London: Harvill Press, 1952). © 1952 by Harvill Press. Reprinted by permission.

Dostoevsky by John Jones (Oxford: Clarendon Press, 1983). © 1983 by Clarendon Press. Reprinted by permission of Oxford University Press.

Dostoevsky and Suicide by N. N. Shneidman (Oakville: Mosaic Press, 1984). © 1984. Reprinted by permission of Mosaic Press.

Resurrection from the Underground by René Girard, trans. James G. Williams (New York: Crossroad Publishing, 1997). © 1997 by René Girard. Reprinted by permission.

Excerpt from *Eleven Essays in the European Novel* by Richard P. Blackmur, Copyright © 1964 and renewed by Elizabeth Blackmur, reprinted by permission of Harcourt, Inc.

The Structure of The Brothers Karamazov by Robert L. Belknap (The Hague: Mouton, 1967). © 1967 by Mouton. Reprinted by permission.

Dostoyevsky: An Examination of the Major Novels by Richard Peace (Cambridge: Cambridge University Press, 1971). © 1971 by Richard Peace. Reprinted by permission.

Dostoyevsky: The Novel of Discord by Malcolm V. Jones (London: Paul Elek, 1976). © 1976 by Paul Elek. Reprinted by permission.

Jackson, Robert Louis. *The Art of Dostoevsky: Deliriums and Nocturnes.* © 1981 by Princeton University Press. Reprinted by permission of Princeton University Press.

"Alyosha Karamazov and the Hagiographic Hero" by Valentina A. Vetlovskaya. From *Dostoevsky: New Perspectives,* Robert Louis Jackson, ed. (Englewood Cliffs: Prentice-Hall, 1984). © 1984 by Prentice Hall. Reprinted by permission.

Dostoevsky: Myths of Duality by Roger B. Anderson (Gainesville: University of Florida Press, 1986). © 1986 by the University of Florida Press. Reprinted by permission of the University Press of Florida.

Index of Themes and Ideas

BROTHERS KARAMAZOV, THE, 14, 70–90; Agrafena Alexandrovna Svetlov (Grushenka) in, 70–72, 74, 76–77, 87; Alexei Fyodorovich Karamazov (Alyosha) in, 14, 70, 71, 72, 73, 74, 76, 77, 78, 79, 81, 82, 83, 86–88; as allegory and psychological novel, 72–73, 78–79; characters in, 74–75; critical views on, 10, 12, 76–90; delay in operation of grace in, 78; Dimitri Fyodorovich Karamazov in, 70, 71–72, 74, 76–77, 78, 79, 80–81; Dmitri's punishment in, 80–81; Epilogue in, 72–73; Fyodor Pavlovich Karamazov in, 11, 70–72, 74, 76–77, 88–90; Grand Inquisitor in, 71, 77, 78, 81–83, 85; guilt in, 72–73, 76–77, 78; Ilyusha Snegiryov in, 72, 73, 75, 78, 86; Ivan Fyodorovich Karamazov in, 70, 71, 72, 73, 74, 76, 77, 78, 79, 80, 81, 82, 83, 84–86; Katerina Ivanova Verkhovtsev in, 70, 71, 72, 75, 76, 78, 79; lamentation and Ivan's repudiation of God in, 84–86; narrative awareness in, 78–79; Oedipal themes in, 12; Pavel Fyodorovich Smerdyakov in, 12, 70, 72, 74–75, 76, 77, 78, 79; plot summary of, 70–73; Zosima in, 70, 71, 73, 75, 77, 78–79, 80, 81, 84, 87, 88–90

CRIME AND PUNISHMENT, 13, 15–37; Alyona Ivanovna in, 15, 16, 24, 25, 26, 27; antinomy in, 29–31; carnival in, 31–33; characters in, 19–20; Christian pagan symbols in, 21–23; critical views on, 9–11, 12, 21–37; Dunya in, 15, 16, 17, 19, 26; Epilogue in, 18, 21–23, 31; Iago in, 10–11, 36; Luzhin in, 16, 17, 20, 28; Marmeladov in, 15, 16, 19, 23, 24, 25, 26, 33; narrator in, 27–29; Petersburg in, 32; plot summary of, 15–18, 23–25; Porfiry as double of Raskolnikov in, 33–35; Porfiry Petrovich in, 16, 17, 20, 30–31, 33–35; Pulcheria Alexandrovna in, 19, 25; Raskolnikov in, 10, 11, 12, 15–17, 18, 19, 21–27, 28–29, 30–31, 32, 33–35, 36–37, 65, 67; Raskolnikov's relationship with women and his dream of beating mare in, 15–16, 25–27; Razumikhin in, 16, 17, 19, 33; reader as one with Raskolnikov's thoughts in, 29–31; and redemption of Raskolnikov, 21–23; Sonya in, 10, 15, 16–17, 18, 19, 21–22, 24, 26, 29, 31, 36; Svidrigailov as Christian failure and existential success in, 36–37; Svidrigailov in, 9–10, 11, 15, 16, 17, 19, 24, 33, 36–37, 50, 66, 67; yellow in, 16

DEMONS (POSSESSED, THE), 13, 53–71; and "At Tikhon's" chapter, 54, 63–65; characters in, 57–58; critical views on, 11, 59–69; Darya (Dasha) in, 53, 54, 55, 58; Fedka in, 54, 55, 58; Kirillov in, 54, 55, 56, 57, 59, 65–67; Lebyadkin in, 53, 54, 55, 58; Liputin in, 58; Liza Tushina in, 53, 54, 55, 58; Marya Timofeyevna in, 53, 54, 55, 58, 61–64; narrator in, 53; Nikolai Stavrogin in, 11, 50, 53–54, 55, 57, 59, 61–63, 63, 67, 68–69; Peter Verhovensky (Stepanovich) in, 53, 54–55, 56, 57, 59, 60, 66–67, 69; plot summary of, 53–56; and Russian political history, 59–61; Shatov in, 53, 54, 55, 57, 59, 67; Stepan Tromfimovitch (Verkhovensky) in, 53, 54, 55, 56, 57, 59–61, 69; suicide and freedom in, 65–67; Varvara Petrovna in, 53–54, 55, 57; Virginsky in, 54, 58

DOSTOEVSKY, FYODOR: biography of, 12–14; Shakespearean Daemonic in, 9–11

DOUBLE, THE, 12

ETERNAL HUSBAND, THE, 13

GAMBLER, THE, 13

HOUSE OF THE DEAD, THE, 13

IDIOT, THE, 13, 38–52; Adelaida in, 42; Afnasy Ivanovitch Totsky in, 38, 42, 44, 45; Aglaya in, 40, 42, 45, 48, 72; Alexandra in, 38, 42; characters in, 42–43; Christian view of time in, 48–50; critical views on, 44–52; execution, epilepsy, and apocalypse in, 39, 46–49; Ferdyshchenko in, 38, 43; Ganya in, 38, 39, 42; General Ivolgin in, 42; General Yepanchin in, 38, 42; Hippolit Terentyev in, 39, 43; Keller in, 43; Kolya in, 42; Lizaveta Prokofyevna in, 12; Lukyan Timmofeyitch Lebedev in, 38, 43; Madam Terentyev in, 43; Myshkin in, 12, 38–39, 40, 41, 42, 45, 46–49, 50–52, 70; Nastasya Filippovna in, 38–39, 40, 42, 44–46, 49; Nina Alexandrovna in, 42; plot summary of, 38–41; Prince S in, 42; Ptitsyn in, 42; Rogozhin in, 38, 39, 40, 41, 42, 45, 47, 49, 50; symbol clusters in, 49; and unconscious, 50–51; Varya in, 40, 42; Vera Lebedev in, 43

INSULTED AND INJURED, THE, 13

NOTES FROM THE UNDERGROUND, 13

POOR FOLK, 12

RAW YOUTH, A, 14

"UNCLE'S DREAM," 12

"VILLAGE OF STEPANCHIKOVO, THE," 13

Fyodor Dostoevsky

DEC 2002